St[...]

To a great
Trojan. Hope
you enjoy all
the wonderful
history here —

Fight On —

Dan

MIRACLE MOMENTS IN
USC TROJANS FOOTBALL
HISTORY

BEST PLAYS, GAMES, AND RECORDS

DAN WEBER

SPORTS
PUBLISHING

Sports Publishing books may be purchased in bulk at special discounts for sales promotion, corporate gifts, fund-raising, or educational purposes. Special editions can also be created to specifications. For details, contact the Special Sales Department, Sports Publishing, 307 West 36th Street, 11th Floor, New York, NY 10018 or sportspubbooks@skyhorsepublishing.com.

Sports Publishing® is a registered trademark of Skyhorse Publishing, Inc.®, a Delaware corporation.

Visit our website at www.sportspubbooks.com.

10 9 8 7 6 5 4 3 2 1

Library of Congress Cataloging-in-Publication Data is available on file.

Cover design by Tom Lau
Cover photo credit AP Images

Interior photos by Long Photography, Kathe Osborne, Dan Avila, Sam Hawthorne, Kirby Lee, and John McGillen (courtesy of USC's Sports Information Department), except where noted.

ISBN: 978-1-68358-246-5
Ebook ISBN: 978-1-68358-247-2

Printed in China

Contents

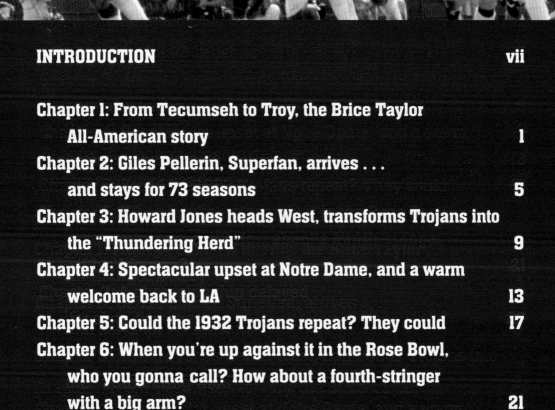

INTRODUCTION

It's a story—or many of them—worthy of Hollywood. The miracle moments that USC football history has produced would easily provide the plot lines for all sorts of big-screen extravaganza treatment.

And they're all true. No one has to make them up.

Here are a number that tell of the people who breathed life into USC football, who took it to the top, who set the standards, who won national championships and Heisman Trophies and Rose Bowls and the hearts of the fans of a growing Southern California just ready to burst into America's cultural consciousness from the booming 1920s on.

USC football was right there every step of the way: from matchups against the Thundering Herd to two separate Wild Bunches (1969 and 2003), from Antelope Al to Jaguar Jon, from Iron Mike to Prince Hal, from Cotton to Thunder & Lightning, Trojans football has been on the tip of the tongue for SoCal fans and beyond. Ironically, the lone program in college football history never to have put the players' names on the backs of their jerseys because it's all about the team would produce so many whose names we all can recall.

But it wouldn't do so right away. The team they were calling the Methodists or the Wesleyans played its first football game in 1888, after Professor Elmer Merrill suggested to Henry Goddard, USC's first coach who had played football himself in college, that they "teach these boys some football." It was 19 years after Rutgers and Princeton had played the first college football game in 1869 that the sport reached Los Angeles.

Yet it was hardly special. At the turn of the century, for just one example, USC was shut out the first five times it faced the Sherman Indian Institute from nearby Riverside by a total score of 72–0 in four losses and a scoreless tie. And when it went in search of a new nickname in 1912, asking the *Los Angeles Times* sports editor Owen Bird for help, he gave it to them. He came up with "Trojans," he said, with an explanation for USC's competitive issues at the time.

"The athletes and coaches of the university were under terrific handicaps," the USC football media guide quotes Bird's reasoning. "They were facing teams that were bigger and better equipped, yet they had splendid fighting spirit. The name 'Trojans' fitted them."

It certainly fit USC's first All-American, lineman Brice Taylor, one of college football's few African-Americans to earn such honors in the game's first eight decades. An orphan adopted by Italian-Americans and a descendant of the great Indian chief Tecumseh, the Seattle native overcame one other hurdle. He was born without a left hand, limiting the speedy athlete to playing on the line. But a lineman fast enough to run on USC's world-record 400-meter relay team had certain advantages, as Taylor served as a transition to what was to come next for USC football.

USC had been no match for a national powerhouse on the West Coast like Cal, a team USC beat just once in their first ten meetings. And then the world turned. Within a year's time in 1922 and 1923, the incredibly optimistic citizens of Pasadena and then Los Angeles built a pair of the world's iconic sporting venues geared to football—the Rose Bowl and the Los Angeles Memorial Coliseum.

Imagine that. With a population of no more than 550,000 in the mid-1920s, Greater LA would have two new stadiums that would ultimately seat 100,000 each; one would host the bowl game that became the "Grand-Daddy of them all," and the other venue will soon become (in 2028) the first ever to host three Summer Olympics, not to mention twelve national champion football teams, including a Trojans team that would dominate the Rose Bowl, plus a place where they play a World Series and host two NFL teams, a president, and a Pope.

With one of the world's great stadiums just across the street from its campus, USC would get on board and, buying out Coach Elmer "Gloomy Gus" Henderson and after a 9–2–0 season and failing to lure Knute Rockne from Notre Dame, would do the next best thing and entice Hall of Famer Howard Jones. An All-American and one-time coach at Yale, Jones headed west from Iowa at Rockne's suggestion. That move would change college football on the West Coast and in the nation forever.

Not only would the Trojans soon be dispatching Cal and Stanford, they would install Notre Dame and Rockne as a schedule fixture, a move that solidified both programs in the firmament of college football, especially when the likes of Michigan and Ohio State were shunning private school Notre Dame. The nation responded. The first two times USC and

Notre Dame met in 1927 and 1929, 120,000 turned out for the first game, 112,912 for the second. Both LA games drew capacity crowds of more than 72,000 at the Coliseum.

But college football's greatest intersectional series would do more than draw fans: it would set up the two teams as the measure for college football excellence, as no one but USC (in 1928, 1931, and 1932) and Notre Dame (in 1929 and 1930—in Rockne's last game) would win a national championship for those five straight seasons. A decade later, USC would be facing a similar situation with the loss of Jones, to a heart attack, after the 1940 season and his teams' four national championships and a perfect 5–0 record in the Rose Bowl.

Getting back to the Howard Jones Era would not come easily. There were occasional highlights, like the day in 1956 when USC running back C.R. Roberts would not only help desegregate Austin, Texas, and the Southwest Conference, but he'd put up a record-breaking day in a win over the Longhorns.

Still, twenty-three middling seasons would go by before a young son of a tiny West Virginia coal town would show USC the way. John McKay had put in his WWII service as a B-29 tail-gunner and physical instructor, then returned to play football at Purdue and Oregon, where as an assistant coach, he attracted the Trojans' interest. But it took some luck for the wise-cracking, cigar-smoking McKay to survive into his third season after opening with a pair of losing seasons and an 8–11–1 record.

But survive he did. And then in 1962, it happened—a national championship and a win in the most wide-open, action-packed Rose Bowl ever to that time, 42–37, over Wisconsin. Another triumphant Trojans era had begun. By the time he would leave for Tampa Bay and the NFL in 1976, McKay's Trojans won four national titles, just like Jones, along with five Rose Bowl wins in eight tries.

McKay's accomplishments didn't end there. There was a 1970 game in segregated Birmingham, Alabama, against an all-white Alabama team coached by his good friend Bear Bryant that would help change the world of college football, as USC, with three African-American starters in the backfield led by sophomore Sam "Bam" Cunningham, would make the case that race should never be a limiting factor.

There were comebacks against Notre Dame, one of them so spectacular it would be labeled simply as "The Comeback," as the Trojans, down 24–0 in the first half, would reverse course like nothing else that college football had ever seen, scoring fifty-five points in less than seventeen minutes for a 55–24 win against the Irish.

There would be a 1972 national championship team so dominant, it's on every list of the best-ever college football teams.

There would be the first two of USC's six—or seven, depending on how you count Reggie Bush—Heisman Trophy winners: Mike Garrett (in 1965) and O.J. Simpson

(1968). That "Tailback U." legacy would continue through McKay's top assistant, John Robinson, who would take over in 1976 and win the 1978 national championship and produce two Heisman winners in three seasons—Charles White (1979) and the incomparable Marcus Allen (1981), the first college player to rush for more than 2,000 yards in a single season.

But with Robinson following McKay into the NFL after the 1982 season, USC would fall into another of those tailspins separating national championship eras. Four coaches, including Robinson for a forgettable five-year return, would preside over eighteen seasons with four of them producing nonwinning records and a 3–2 mark in five Rose Bowls. Even worse, there were just three Top Ten finishes and no Heisman winners during that time.

Sure, there would be a Keyshawn Johnson and a 41–32 Rose Bowl win over a plucky Northwestern team in 1996, but that was about it. USC football had hit a flat spot.

Then along came Pete Carroll. Rejected by the NFL's Patriots and Jets, with a daughter at USC, and a year to think things over, Carroll was USC's fourth choice. This was not a job the world wanted. But Carroll would change all that—in a heartbeat, as they say. Despite having run out of running backs in a season that began with just two wins in the first seven games, USC would finish in a rush with a 27–0 win over No. 20 UCLA to earn a spot in the Las Vegas Bowl and a 6–6 finish.

But that was just a start. With quarterback Carson Palmer and safety Troy Polamalu back to lead them, the No. 4 Trojans would rout UCLA, Notre Dame, and No. 3 Iowa, 38–17, in the Orange Bowl to signal their return to the top. And it would not stop there.

On teams led by five All-American defenders—Kenechi Udeze, Shaun Cody, Matt Grootegoed, Lofa Tatupu, and Mike Patterson—another Heisman winner would emerge. Quarterback Matt Leinart would lead the Trojans to two straight national titles in 2003 and 2004 and thirty-four straight wins that took them within nineteen seconds of an unprecedented third in a row when the defense ran out in the 2006 Rose Bowl to Texas and Vince Young's Texas Longhorns.

By the time Carroll headed back to the NFL after the 2010 season, he went with a record of five Rose Bowl wins in six tries along with two Orange Bowl wins including one titanic BCS national championship game there with a 55–19 romp over Oklahoma. Carroll helped lead three Heisman winners in four seasons with Palmer (2002), Leinart (2004), and Bush, who later returned his trophy after NCAA sanctions in 2010 declared him ineligible in 2005.

As it proved in the past when national championship coaches leave, the aftermath would not go easily for USC. With two of Carroll's young offensive coordinators— Lane Kiffin and Steve Sarkisian—coming next as head coaches, USC would struggle, save for

Kiffin's bowl-restricted 10–2 season in 1911. But at least life would not be boring after Pete.

For the first time in major college football history, a school would be forced to fire two coaches in mid-season just two years apart. Kiffin would be axed in 2013 at LAX after returning from an embarrassing loss at Arizona State and Sarkisian in 2015 after several embarrassing episodes—one at a team booster function and the second at a practice for which Sarkisian was sent home unable to coach. And still, USC wasn't awful despite NCAA sanctions that took away two bowl games and 30 scholarships and forced the Trojans to show up with as few as 43 originally recruited scholarship players for games against teams that could have as many as 85.

In one of the craziest seasons in college football history, USC would have three head coaches in 2013, with Ed Orgeron succeeding Kiffin and subsequently leaving after Sarkisian was hired after the end of the regular season, when Clay Helton took over as interim coach for the Las Vegas Bowl. Counting Sarkisian's December hire, that's four coaches in one calendar year. The multicoach season was repeated in 2015, when Sarkisian was fired after five games for "conduct not up to the standard of a USC head coach" and Helton took over for the final seven games before being named head coach for the 2016 season.

Despite the fact the Helton led the Trojans to a win at the Rose Bowl after the 2016 season and USC's first Pac-12 title in 2017, many fans will tell you that the jury is still out on Helton despite a 27–10 mark, nine Top 25 wins, and victories in more games (21) in his first two seasons than any other USC head coach. The wins over Penn State and Washington's College Football Playoff team in 2016 and the two wins over Stanford in 2017 are very much on the plus side for Helton. The routs at Notre Dame and in the Cotton Bowl, and the upset at Washington State, are not.

How Helton will handle the loss of Sam Darnold, Ronald Jones, and Deontay Burnett for 2018 is the question of the moment. But USC football is much more than any one season. The program that has produced 166 first-team All-Americans, more NFL first-round picks than any other program, and is tied for the most No. 1 overall draft picks will not be defined by any one season.

More than likely, it will be defined by the kinds of records that USC football seems to inspire. Like the way "Superfan" Giles Pellerin attended 797 straight USC games over eight decades, a record without challenge across all of college football. Or how the USC Marching Band has appeared at 389 straight Trojans games, traveling to every Trojan road game the last 30 seasons, another record unchallenged in college football.

Then, of course, there's Jake Olson, the Trojans' blind long-snapper who was two for two in 2017 in perfect snaps and USC's Most Inspirational Player. The story of the young Trojans football fan who lost his sight to cancer surgery a day after attending his last USC practice at the age of twelve and then returned to practice with and play for his favorite team is one of college football's most memorable moments.

This is USC football. And these are its Miracle Moments.

1

From Tecumseh to Troy, the Brice Taylor All-American Story

It is one of the most honored spots on the campus at the University of Southern California: the Trojan All-American Walk leading from the McKay Center, home of the football team, to the practice field complex across McClintock Way. There are 166 first-team USC football All-Americans enshrined—and pictured—there for the current Trojans to walk by and acknowledge.

But there is only one inaugural USC All-American there—a Trojan whose story has yet to be equaled in the 82 years since Brice Taylor earned his place on the wall.

For most of its existence, USC football has had a Hollywood connection like no other program in the nation. Some of its greatest early stars, like late-1920s captain Ward Bond, excelled at USC before going on to great success in movies and TV. Bond was a member of the Trojans teams that captured their first-ever national championships in 1928, 1931, and 1932. Another Trojan and Bond's buddy, Marion Morrison (a.k.a. John Wayne), didn't stay at USC long enough to become a football star but had even more success when Hollywood called to cast him.

But USC's original All-American star, Brice Taylor, seems to have come straight out of central casting almost before the movie industry—or USC football—got going. Back in 1923, out of Seattle's Franklin High School, Taylor came down the West Coast to Los Angeles to school. "[He] ought to be a movie," then-*Newsday* sports columnist Chuck Culpepper wrote of Taylor in 2006.

Brice had it all—or almost all. An African-American as well as a direct descendent of the famed Shawnee Indian chief Tecumseh, Brice was raised by an adoptive family of Italian immigrants. But there was something else that made Brice unique, especially on the football field—Brice had been born without a left hand. So he would have to play on the line of scrimmage in college despite his relatively small stature and terrific speed.

"Hey, you try running the ball with one hand," he would respond when it was suggested he give running back the old college try. But he never made much of it unless pressed. "He never talked about it and unless you looked, you'd never know," Brad Pye Jr., one of his former students and players at Los Angeles Jefferson High who went on to be sports editor at the black-owned *Los Angeles Sentinel,* told *Newsday's* Culpepper in 2006.

As for carrying the football, Brice had done it in high school, leading the Franklin team he captained to the 1922 Washington state championship as a running back before being named Washington's High School Athlete of the Year. So he may have just been downplaying what he could do. In high school, he even played baseball. And reports from the players he coached at LA's Jefferson High suggested that he could throw and catch with anybody.

He was versatile, to say the least. At USC, he kicked off and was a tough defender in addition to playing offensive guard. But more than anything, he could run. One report in the *LA Times* had Brice, at 5-foot-9 and 185 pounds, running the 100-yard dash in the world-class time of 9.9 seconds. He may well have been the only All-American football lineman to be a member of a world-record-setting mile relay team, as he was at USC. "Although he was a guard, he was as fast as the backs in those days," fullback C.R. Roberts, a 1956 star, told Culpepper.

Brice was also a hurdler at USC. And yes, he had more than his share of hurdles. Only five African-Americans had been named All-American before the Football Writers of America selected Brice in 1925, the first year he played for Jones, after the Trojans finished 11–2 that season. Even in Los Angeles, which would produce a Jackie Robinson nearly two decades later at UCLA, Brice was not immune to racism. Numerous reports have stated that he would hear catcalls from the stands about his race. And after Brice, USC would not produce another African-American All-American for nearly four decades, until 1964 when "Iron Mike" Garrett, who would win the Heisman Trophy in 1965, earned the honor.

As the USC Black Alumni Association noted in honoring Brice: "He was an African-American All-American forty years before Jim Crow laws were painstakingly laid to rest. He was an African-American All-American four years before Martin Luther King Jr. was even born. Taylor was not just battling slurs from hostile road crowds, he was thriving in an era of institutionalized racism. And, by all accounts nearly a century later, he did it with a smile on his face."

USC was not immune to those times, as the University did not list Brice as an All-American in its media guides until the 1950s. It took a campaign by Pye and friends to get Taylor's All-American honor listed there. Although by 1995, seventy years after his All-American season and 21 years after his death, Taylor was inducted into the second class of the USC Athletics Hall of Fame.

Looking back now, it seems that Brice had always been there for USC. He helped kick off college football's greatest intersectional rivalry in 1925 in the recently built LA Memorial Coliseum, which hosted the first-ever USC-Notre Dame game, a 13–12 loss to Knute Rockne's Irish. USC would finish 26–8 over Brice's three seasons and defeat Missouri in the 1925 Christmas Festival Bowl game at the Coliseum. That same season three weeks earlier, Brice took part in USC's first-ever Homecoming game as the Trojans hosted Syracuse.

Brice Taylor managed to overcome so much in his life as the youngest of 10 children of Cyrus Taylor, a bricklayer. But he was orphaned at age five. Fortunately for Brice, the DiJulio family in Seattle took him in. After his star-studded high school days in Seattle, reports are that he had 17 college scholarship offers from East Coast schools and eight more from the West Coast, but none from the school he wanted to attend in his hometown, the University of Washington.

Then along came USC football coach "Gloomy Gus" Henderson with a scholarship offer to attend USC, just as the Trojans were getting going. It turned out to be a great move for USC, getting a player who could run, block, tackle, and contribute as a kicker on special teams. "I met him about 1931 when I was playing at USC," Julius Bescos told Culpepper. "And he came to practice. And Howard Jones introduced him to the group . . . They said he would take on tackles and he would just demolish them because he was so quick and strong."

Brice's first stop after graduation was Baton Rouge, Louisiana, where he became the head football coach and athletic director at Southern University. It was there that, in 1931, Taylor would lead the school to its first undefeated football season. But Brice would do something else for America's Historically Black Colleges and Universities (HBCU) before he left: he would put a small-town northwest Louisiana school by the name of Louisiana Negro Normal and Industrial Institute on the Southern schedule. And much like the USC-Notre Dame series, the two schools—Southern and the now Grambling State University—would grow their annual series into the famed Bayou Classic.

That was hardly the end of it for Brice as a college administrator. In 1939, he would become the president of Guadalupe College, a small Baptist school in Seguin in South Texas for African-American students that was trying to survive a major fire and the impact of the economy at the end of the Depression.

But several years earlier, in 1931, Brice had left Baton Rouge to return home, and in doing so became the first-ever African-American head football coach at a Los Angeles High

School. He was also a physical education teacher. Through those years, Brice invested in LA real estate, earned a doctorate in theology, and served as a minister for more than four decades for the First African Methodist Episcopal Church in Los Angeles.

And just to show the kind of Renaissance man he was, under Brice, the first high school tennis program in Los Angeles was started at Jefferson, and one of the players on that first team, Oscar Johnson, went on in 1948 to become the first black athlete to win an integrated USLTA tournament (the Long Beach Junior Open) on his way to induction into the International Tennis Hall of Fame in 1987.

"He was real strict, but he was fair," Pye recalled. "For me, he was bigger than life. I had read about him. He was SC's first All-American. I think we all were afraid of him."

To the end, Brice Taylor was Cardinal and Gold all the way, Pye said. "Yeah, he was a Trojan. I couldn't understand his loyalty to USC because of the way black athletes were just ignored." But a Trojan Taylor was to the very end. After visiting him in 1974 at a nursing home in Downey shortly before his death at the age of seventy-two, Pye noticed how Taylor would greet everyone he met with one Trojan reference or another.

Now Brice Taylor greets every Trojan—All-American or not—on USC's Trojan All-American Walk from his No. 1 spot at the head of the line, where he so deserves to be. After all, USC was more than lucky to have him come along ninety-five years ago to set the tone for so much that would follow in Trojans football history.

2

Giles Pellerin, Superfan, arrives . . . and stays for 73 seasons

All he ever wanted to be, once he got going, was "USC's No. 1 fan."

Or maybe "the No. 1 Trojan."

But in his more than eight decades of following his beloved Trojans, Giles Pellerin became much more than that. He was named college football's first-ever Sears DieHard Fan for the NCAA's Division I. And it wasn't even a close contest—nor will it ever be.

His moments are many, as are the miracles attached to them.

That number, we can say, only starts at 797—as in 797 straight USC football games that Pellerin attended, home and away, all over the nation. Of course, this was back in the days before interstates, jet planes, and almost before planes themselves!

The number is so ridiculously outside the realm of possibility, it will never be challenged. Think of that. It's one of those records you can write in the record book and forget about. No one's getting there.

From that day in 1926 as a USC sophomore when he watched his Trojans crush Whittier, 74–0, at the Coliseum to that day in 1998 when he died with his boots on at the age of ninety-one, after suffering a heart attack at the halftime of the USC-UCLA game in the parking lot of the Rose Bowl, Giles never missed a beat.

Giles Pellerin

5

Not once. And the close calls were many, as one might expect in seventy-three seasons.

"God must be a Trojan, I've been lucky," he said of the way he managed to keep his streak in an era before transcontinental air travel—and even before Charles Lindbergh's famous flight. Furthermore, Pellerin was following a team from LA, where the USC alum with an electrical engineering degree and a career as a telephone company executive was often thousands of miles away from many of the Trojans' road games.

The estimates are that Giles spent $100,000 (not adjusted to today's dollars) in traveling more than 650,000 miles to USC road games and saw the Trojans' record reach 532–225–40, with more than 120 All-Americans in tow. "Giles lived and breathed USC football," said his younger brother, Oliver, who put together his own streak of 637 games from 1945 to 2001.

That first year, Giles went to Cal in Berkeley and Portland, Oregon, for the Oregon State game. The next year, it was off to Chicago's Soldier Field as part of what many believe was the largest crowd in college football history—120,000—where the Trojans took on Knute Rockne's Irish.

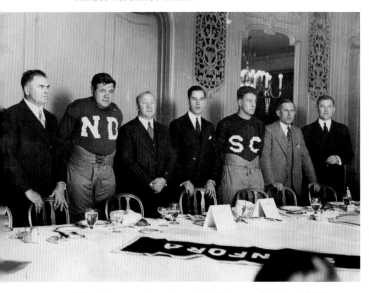

The pregame luncheon in Chicago for the 1927 USC-Notre Dame game that would draw 120,000 at Soldier Field the next day. Among those pictured are coach Knute Rockne (third from left), Babe Ruth (second from left), Lou Gehrig (third from right), and USC coach Howard Jones (second from right). All four would be named Hall of Famers in their sport.

During the early seasons, USC played most of its games at home. Then Washington, Washington State, and Pittsburgh became part of the road schedule, as well as Hawaii for two games in 1936, which caused Giles famously to put off his honeymoon for eight months.

Illinois and Ohio State road trips came in those pre-WWII years to the Midwest, then Tulane after the war, then Army at Yankee Stadium, Texas, Wisconsin, Michigan, Baylor, Southern Methodist, Oklahoma, and Michigan State a week apart, then Miami (Fla.), Minnesota, Iowa, Nebraska, and in that game that so impacted civil rights in the South and all of America, Alabama in Birmingham to open the 1970 season. There, an integrated USC team helped Paul "Bear" Bryant prepare Alabama and the rest of the Deep South for the arrival of African-American players to their schools and the game of college football.

By then, Giles was flying on the USC charter, and life was considerably more convenient for a man who belonged there as much as any player or coach. "I think of all the USC players as part of my family," said the man who had no children of his own.

He flew to Purdue and Missouri, Texas Tech and LSU, Tennessee and Indiana, Boston College and Syracuse, Penn State, Houston, and Florida State in that last season.

As Steve Bisheff and Loel Schrader document so well in their book *Fight On: The Colorful Story of USC Football*, Giles made it clear how he felt: "I never played the game but I love it," he said.

"There's just a certain spirit about college football. I've always said that going to USC games is the thing that has kept me alive, young, and happy. . . . Some people think I'm crazy for spending as much money as I have traveling to see these games. They don't understand that I do more than watch a game when I visit these cities. I've met a lot of nice and interesting people on these trips. Sure, I could sit in my rocking chair and grow old. But I don't intend to do that. You've got to have something to look forward to."

One of those people Giles met, in 1989, was yours truly, then the director of the Traveling College Football Hall of Fame, as we visited South Bend for the USC-Notre Dame game. In our customized RV that was parked next to the host stadium and served as a miniaturized College Football Hall of Fame, it was customary to have thousands of fans come through during the weekend. Some of them would linger and talk college football.

Giles and Oliver were two members of their group of five USC fans. The more we talked, the more Giles's role as the instructor became clear. No matter the topic, Giles had been there, done that and could give a graduate course on just about anything in college football history. Only as the Pellerins left did one of their companions let me know who Giles was and from where he had come.

But even then, Giles did not tell those amazing stories of how he kept the streak—and himself—alive. Like how in 1993, when a ruptured abdominal aneurism struck him leaving his hotel in Harrisburg, Pennsylvania, and he was hospitalized for 12 days. But the streak went on. USC had a bye the next week, and as the story goes, he signed himself out of the hospital with a waiver that they weren't responsible and high-tailed it home for that Saturday's Washington State game.

Someone was watching out for Giles. As Bisheff and Schrader note, he survived an emergency appendectomy five days before a game in 1949 and a blown water pump on his drive to South Bend the day before a game.

In the *USC Trojans Football Encyclopedia*, Richard J. Shmelter details the appendectomy story. According to Shmelter, Pellerin was up and moving around the hospital that Saturday when USC was hosting Oregon and asked the nurses if he could take a walk. They granted him permission to do so, but what he didn't tell them was that he would be walking from his car to the Coliseum for the game, a 40–13 USC win, and then return to the hospital. This took place without the nurses ever knowing he was gone.

Twenty years later, he had a tumor removed from his stomach during the summer, requiring six weeks of bed rest. Sorry, Giles said when the Trojans opened at Nebraska—he was there. In fact, he was always there.

And he still is. By the time he'd finished his run that day at the Rose Bowl, Giles had donated $1 million for athletic scholarships that live to this very day and then he willed $2 million in investments and his home to the university.

So the numbers are much higher than 797.

Nevertheless, you can record this author as seconding the suggestion of Bisheff and Schrader: that the number 797 in bright Cardinal and Gold be memorialized in a prominent place at the LA Memorial Coliseum.

After all, even before the streak, it's the place that Giles started his fandom as a high school student in 1924 when he showed up as one of 47,000 fans for USC's first bowl game, the Christmas Festival, a 20–7 December 25 win over Missouri. No one has mattered more there than Giles Pellerin, USC Superfan.

3

Howard Jones heads West, transforms Trojans into the "Thundering Herd"

It took Howard Jones almost no time to work his miracle ways upon his arrival in Los Angeles in 1925. And maybe that should have come as no surprise. The former Yale All-American, at the age of forty-one, had already been the head coach at Syracuse (1908), Yale (1909, 1913), Ohio State (1910), Iowa (1916–1923), and Duke (1924).

He'd won three national titles as a player at Yale and one as a coach there in 1909. And so it made sense for USC, after buying out the contract of Elmer "Gloomy Gus" Henderson, who posted a 45–7 record after six years, because he couldn't beat Cal, to bring a coach with Jones's record to fill the recently built Los Angeles Memorial Coliseum.

There was another reason to bring in Jones after it was reported that USC made an attempt to hire Notre Dame's Knute Rockne, which fell short when the story got out that USC had met with the legendary Irish coach. With Jones came his Ivy League résumé, and for a

USC Coach Howard Jones, pictured with captain Don McNeil, in 1938.
Associated Press

USC program that was taking shots from both Cal and Stanford for its supposed academic shortcomings, Yale grad and former coach Jones appeared to be the perfect response.

But in 1928, there was a different Bay Area challenge for USC football. The Trojans had never defeated the legendary Glenn "Pop" Warner and his Stanford team, and it looked like it would be another one of those years when the mighty Indians showed up that November 3 day in LA. A standing-room-only crowd of 80,000 fans waited at the Coliseum to cheer on the unbeaten Trojans, who had a 0–0 tie against Cal in an earlier game at Berkeley, where the no-grass, all-sand field had reportedly been mysteriously wet and impossible to play on, despite no rain in a game where USC rang up fifteen first downs to Cal's five.

USC, after all, was getting closer to Stanford after managing a 13–13 tie a year earlier in Palo Alto.

But this was different. This was the moment when the five-time-national-champion Howard Jones showed exactly why he would be inducted into the College Football Hall of Fame in its inaugural 1951 class as one of the all-time greats in college football history.

This was the moment at which USC lived up to what is now their current nickname—and the name that *LA Times* sports editor Owen Bird conferred on the team previously called the Methodists, the Wesleyans, and the Puritans, until that 1912 track meet against Stanford when Bird came up with it—the Trojans. As Steven Travers references in *Trojans Essential*, Bird would go on to explain, "The term 'Trojan' as applied to USC means to me that no matter what the situation, what the odds or what the conditions, the competition must be carried on to the end and those who strive must give all they have and never be weary in doing so."

True to what would become their fight song, the Trojans did indeed "Fight On," proving themselves to be a team that would become nationally dominant almost in an eye-blink. For on that November day, against a Stanford team that Warner considered his best ever, they would win—and win convincingly. (As a footnote, they would never lose to Warner's Stanford teams again after this 10–0 USC win.)

USC would accomplish the feat with a "quick mix" swarming defense, as they called it, led by physical play up front from All-American tackle and captain Jesse Hibbs that forced five turnovers. Hibbs, an athletic 6-foot, 183-pounder out of Normal, Illinois, and Lake Forest Academy by way of Glendale, had Route 66'ed his way to USC, where he also played basketball before returning to the Midwest to play professionally for the Chicago Bears and another of the great football coaches—George Halas. Hibbs would go on to become a television and movie director, one of a number of USC football players to follow that path after working in the movies as an undergrad at USC.

Hibbs wasn't alone. Freshman defensive end Garrett Arbelbide (6-1, 178) would go on to become a 1930 All-American playing halfback as well as baseball at USC. The Huntington Park product would play on two national championship teams at USC (also in 1931), in two Rose Bowls, and on the first USC team to win at Notre Dame, in 1931.

On offense, that USC team boasted a speedy backfield of Don Williams, Marshall Duffield, and Russ Saunders, who would score the lone touchdown against Stanford on a pitch from Williams. The 5-foot-9, 158-pound Williams, out of Santa Ana, would go on to become a 1928 All-American who led USC in both rushing (681 yards) and scoring (47 points) that season.

Clips of that game reveal how a quicker Trojans team that benefited from an early Stanford fumble on the USC two-yard line would use that break to get a feel for the game—and Stanford. From that point on, USC's speed and toughness against the bigger Indians proved to be the difference in an all-out slug-'em-out game.

Two other eventual All-Americans anchored the "Thundering Herd." Nate Barragar, a 6-foot, 198-pound 1929 All-American center and guard from San Fernando, would go on to play professionally for Minneapolis, Frankford, and Green Bay after his USC career before returning home to become a motion picture producer and director.

Francis Tappaan, a 5-foot-10, 165-pound end from Los Angeles who was also a hockey player at USC, would go on to become an assistant coach for the Trojans and then an attorney, judge, legislative analyst, Department of Justice official, vice president of North American Rockwell, and vice president of student and alumni affairs at USC.

Those five future USC Athletic Hall of Famers, together with Coach Jones, formed the nucleus of a Trojans program that would win two national titles (also in 1931), beat Rockne's Notre Dame team twice including a first-ever win in South Bend (1931), and establish West Coast dominance over previous powers Cal and Stanford.

A season-ending 27–14 win over Notre Dame in front of 72,632 at the Coliseum firmly established that 1928 Trojans team's legacy, thanks to 111 passing yards from Williams. The only thing that team did not accomplish was win a Rose Bowl after USC declined a bid that year and Cal stepped in, only to lose to Georgia Tech.

Turning down the Rose Bowl was a mistake USC would not make again, accepting an invitation after the 1929 season and whipping Pittsburgh, 47–14, with many of these same players. And of course, they had Jones as their coach, and he would win all five of the Rose Bowls in which his Trojans teams would play.

But it started on that day in November 1928, when the "Thundering Herd's" tough defense was too quick and its hang-in-there offense too fast for a never-again-dominant Stanford.

4

Spectacular upset at Notre Dame, and a warm welcome back to LA

The upset was spectacular. The return to Los Angeles even more so. As both should have been.

Sure, USC had been the last team to beat Notre Dame three seasons earlier. And sure, Notre Dame had gone unbeaten in twenty-six straight games since that 27–14 USC win that gave the Trojans their first national championship in 1928. But that was in LA in front of a friendly Coliseum crowd of 72,632.

This one was not. It happened in South Bend in the first year of the stadium that Knute Rockne, himself, had designed before his untimely death in a plane crash in Kansas after the 1930 season.

And here came the Trojans. They'd had one misfire, against St. Mary's in the season opener, losing 13–7. "I have no alibis to offer," Hall of Fame head coach Howard Jones said afterward. But from that point on, in outscoring their next six opponents, 215–6 with five shutouts, the Trojans were rolling.

Yet they rolled only so far as the Ramblers—as Notre Dame teams were called then— hit back, shutting out USC 14–0 heading into the final quarter that November 21 day in front of an official crowd of 50,731, the first capacity crowd in the inaugural year of Notre Dame's new stadium.

And then it happened—as the USC yearbook, *El Rodeo*, called it, "the biggest upset since Mrs. O'Leary's cow knocked over that lantern." After all, it was not supposed to happen here on their home turf, not to this Notre Dame team that had just dedicated its stadium to Rockne.

Notre Dame jumped out to the lead with a fifty-five-yard TD run in the first half and a second score just four plays into the second. But, as multiple accounts of the game suggested, they subsequently fell apart.

USC fans would tell you the Trojans had a big part of that fall although a Notre Dame interference penalty did put the ball at the Ramblers' sixteen-yard line early in the fourth quarter. And that was enough for USC All-American quarterback Gaius "Gus" Shaver to get USC on the board from there, powering it into the end zone. But Notre Dame blocked the extra point and the Trojans trailed, 14–6. Shaver would come back to score again quickly on the next drive, and USC kicker Johnny Baker knocked the extra point through, making it 14–13.

Here's how *Time* magazine's account of this most newsworthy game described it: "What happened after that was so rapid, so out of keeping with what usually happens in Notre Dame games that 52,000 spectators who saw it found it hard to believe."

The 5-foot-11, 185-pound Shaver was the star once more in the final minutes, completing passes for 50 and 23 yards. But then USC decided not to go for the TD; they would go for the win instead. Baker lined up at the twenty-three-yard line and, with a perfect snap and hold, made up for that blocked extra point, kicking a thirty-three-yard field goal perfectly splitting the uprights.

As sportswriter Maxwell Stiles called the finish: "Johnny Baker's ten little toes and three BIG points."

USC 16, Notre Dame 14.

"AT THE FALL OF NOTRE DAME BUT WHAT A BATTLE" is the headline that appeared in the *Chicago Tribune* the next day. "What a battle it had been," the story continues. "USC's four fumbles (two lost) to Notre Dame's none, kept this one close. Ultimately, Notre Dame's ninety yards in penalties, to none for USC, worked very much in USC's favor."

"I've waited two years for this day," USC All-American halfback Erny Pinckert said after the game, "but boy, what revenge."

Nevertheless, the comeback at Notre Dame, spectacular and unexpected as it was the way it played out, turned out to be just the warmup act that weekend for USC football.

Upon arriving back in LA, where the population in 1931 was an estimated 550,000, the Trojans were greeted by an adoring crowd of more than 300,000 fans. Even now, a souvenir program from that USC-Notre Dame game is listed for $499.99 on eBay.

According to the *Los Angeles Daily News*, Baker's field goal, although long gone from most USC fans' memories, is a candidate for one of the top five iconic plays in USC football history. But there's no dispute about where the welcoming festivities ranked when the Trojans arrived back in town. They were pretty much in a class by themselves.

The *Evening Herald*'s front page describes the welcome home for USC's Trojans after their 1931 win at Notre Dame on the way to a national championship.

When the USC team's train reached LA's Union Station, the Trojans discovered the city had set up a parade from City Hall to the USC campus, some three miles away. "No conquering army of Rome ever received a more tumultuous welcome," proclaimed the *Los Angeles Times*.

So taken was LA with these football Trojans, in the next year's Summer Olympic Games at the Coliseum, the chosen "demonstration sport" was American football, the only time American football was ever played in the Olympics.

After the game against Notre Dame, USC would beat Washington (44–7) and Georgia (60–0) at home. The Trojans then headed to the Rose Bowl to face an unbeaten Tulane team that USC would defeat 21–12.

Shaver, out of Alhambra, would rush for 936 yards that season and remains in the USC record book as the twenty-second all-time leading career rusher. He was joined by two-time All-American Erny Pinckert (5-11, 194) out of San Bernardino, who was repeating his 1930 honors. A member of the College Football Hall of Fame and the Rose Bowl Hall of Fame, Pinckert would play professionally for the Boston Braves and the Boston-Washington Redskins until 1940 before going into the clothes designing business.

Guard and place-kicker Baker (5-10, 185), out of Kingsburg, California, but born in Dennison, Iowa, would return to his home state to become head coach at Northern Iowa, then Nebraska-Omaha, Sacramento State, and Sacramento City College as well as athletic director at Sacramento State.

Finally, center Stan Williamson (6-1, 198) out of Pittsburg, California, the captain of that 1931 team, would go on to become an assistant coach at Kansas State and Oklahoma before finishing as a teacher, coach, and athletic director at UC Santa Barbara.

Perhaps Coach Jones summed it up best that season when he referred to his Trojans as "the greatest offensive machine I have ever coached."

5

Could the 1932 Trojans repeat? They could

Sure, USC's Trojans were the new kids on the block, the hot new major program with two national championships in four years after their rise to the top of the West Coast, passing Stanford and Cal along the way.

Yet the million-dollar question as the 1932 season arrived, and after losing seven regulars and three All-Americans from the 1931 national championship team, was could the Trojans do something they'd never accomplished—win back-to-back national titles—especially after losing that much talent?

They could, indeed. In fact, they would make it look easy, even after All-American Orv Mohler went down with an injury. It was almost as if Jones knew what was coming.

With Mohler sidelined for nearly half the 1932 season, USC wouldn't miss a beat because, as Jones had predicted, "if anything happens to him, I have [Homer] Griffith and [Cotton] Warburton."

Indeed, he did. But that USC team had more, much more. And not just in the backfield. And not just the kind of speed and precision that characterized those early USC teams. This Trojans team started up front with three All-Americans—two tackles and a guard—and a fourth front-line player who would become a 1933 All-American.

Start with Ernie Smith, a 6-2, 215-pound tackle out of Gardena who would be USC's first unanimous All-American. The native of Spearfish, South Dakota, would play professionally with Green Bay after college but at USC would lead a defense that shut out its first five opponents—Utah (35–0), Washington State (20–0), Oregon State (10–0), Loyola (6–0) and Stanford (13–0) before allowing Cal to score in the fourth quarter of a 27–7 USC win in Game Six.

USC's 1932 All-American tackle pair of Ernie Smith, left, and Raymond "Tay" Brown.
Associated Press

That became something of a trend for the physical Trojans, who allowed just one more score—to Washington 9–6 in the mud—while shutting out Oregon (33–0), Notre Dame (13–0), and Pittsburgh (35–0) in the Rose Bowl.

Smith didn't succeed alone, though. On the opposite side of the line was tackle—and team captain—Raymond "Tay" Brown (6-0, 204), out of Compton, a College Football Hall of Famer who was a member of the core group of USC players to win two national championships, beat Notre Dame in South Bend, and win two Rose Bowls. A track and field athlete as well, Brown epitomized how athletic these USC teams were up front, with his 1931 USC track team also winning a national championship. After USC, where Brown first became an assistant coach, he moved on to the University of Cincinnati as an assistant football coach and eventually was named head basketball coach there.

Then there were the guards. Aaron Rosenberg (6-0, 210) out of LA's Fairfax High was in the first of his two All-American seasons. During his time at USC, when his teams won all three games against Notre Dame, USC had a 27-game and 25-game win streak. The College Football Hall of Famer would go on, as so many Trojans of that era did, to a career as a television and movie producer.

Guard Larry Stevens (6-2, 205) was the only one of this quartet not to be named a 1932 All-American, but the Piedmont product would make up for it in 1933, when he became an All-American. He would also succeed Brown, USC's 1932 Most Inspirational Player, by winning that award the next season.

That kind of up-front leadership may have made this USC team unbeatable, but it didn't end there. Leading the offense was Irvine "Cotton" Warburton, just 5-foot-6 and 148 pounds, out of San Diego, another versatile athlete who also ran track at USC. But run the football is what he did best, leading USC in rushing in 1932 and 1933. He would go on to earn a place in the College Football Hall of Fame and also in the U.S. Softball Hall of Fame.

Nor was that all the Cotton kid did. Joining so many Trojan alums, Warburton would move into the film industry, earning an Academy Award for his Oscar-winning film editing for the movie *Mary Poppins*.

Rounding out the squad was a backfield directed by Griffith, and with help on the edge from ends Ray Sparling and Ford Palmer.

In totality, Howard Jones's third national championship team in five years and first ever to go back-to-back was his best. It was so good, in fact, that Jones would make the cover of *Time* magazine, which would draw comparisons between Jones and the legendary pair of Amos Alonzo Stagg and Glenn "Pop" Warner. *Athlon* magazine would, in retrospect, say that the 1932 USC team ranked among the very best of the twentieth century.

Nothing they did in 1932 would change that. Those 8–0 Trojans arrived at the regular season finale in a Homecoming game at the Coliseum against Notre Dame, the only thing standing in the way of an unbeaten regular season, as 93,924 fans (although LA *Herald-Examiner* listed the crowd as 101,000) showed up to cheer on their hometown Trojans. And USC did not disappoint, recording their seventh shutout of the season, one that would send them on to the Rose Bowl.

One oddity about this game: despite the defending national champions' record of having allowed just two touchdowns all season, USC was considered the underdog, with Notre Dame considered the betting public's favorite somehow. But Notre Dame Coach

Heartley "Hunk" Anderson disagreed. In fact, two days before the game, he picked USC, by the exact 13–0 score (life was different in those days, and coaches did that sort of thing).

With the shutout win, led by what was called the "whirling dervish" play of 190-pound Trojan quarterback Griffith, as the *Notre Dame Football Review* would describe him, USC finished out a five-year run in which the only teams to win national championships were USC (1928, 1931, and 1932) and Notre Dame—1929 and 1930. USC became the first team to beat Notre Dame in back-to-back seasons since Nebraska did so in 1922 and 1923.

The road to the national championship was not exactly a walk in the park, though. In fact, USC's national championship would come only after the Rose Bowl, where the Trojans faced Jock Sutherland's unbeaten (8–0–2) Pittsburgh Panthers, the other team to beat Notre Dame (by a 12–0 score) that season. The Panthers were out to avenge their school-record 33-point defeat the last time they faced USC in the Rose Bowl, a 47–14 beatdown. But that was not to be.

"The boys from the Alleghenies put up a brave defense early but the Trojans carried too many guns for them," the *New York Times* reported in a story headlined *Southern California wins fourth straight Rose Bowl by record margin, Pitt crushed 35–0 as 83,000 look on.* USC, in winning its twentieth straight game, was too big, too fast, too strong, and too powerful, racking up twenty-two first downs and 288 yards of offense to Pitt's nine and 193, respectively.

"Smart, aggressive and versatile," Sutherland called this USC team, the first ever to win four straight Rose Bowls. "They had too much power for us at the guard and tackle positions." They also had too much "Cotton" Warburton, as USC's speed back ran for two touchdowns to seal a 10–0 season and USC's third national title under Jones.

"A glorious finish to a great season," Jones said, singling out USC's seniors for their work all season.

The Associated Press agreed, noting that "While the contest had no official championship rating, many fans regarded it as a national titular contest." Pitt's Sutherland concurred, saying simply: "Southern California should be regarded as the national champion."

6

When you're up against it in the Rose Bowl, who you gonna call? How about a fourth-stringer with a big arm?

It was the start of the 1938 season, and things were looking like USC football was on a bit of a downward slide. Gone were the All-Americans, and gone were the winning records after that 1933 national championship season. For four years in a row, Howard Jones's Trojans had not won more than five games in a season.

Three national championships in five seasons—and then they were gone. Would they ever get back to where they were, to where the Herd would be thundering to a Rose Bowl once again?

They would indeed, although a disappointing 19–7 home loss to Alabama in the opener in front of 70,000 fans at the Coliseum had folks wondering if the Trojans were really back. But after heading east to Columbus, where they would beat the Buckeyes, 14–7, in front of 62,778, they would sweep the Bay Area schools and beat Oregon in the Portland mud—all the while stumbling just once more, a 7–6 upset by Washington in rainy Seattle. But a strong end to the regular season, including a 42–7 win over UCLA followed by a decisive 13–0 upset of No. 1 Notre Dame with 97,146 Coliseum fans cheering them on, rocketed the 8–2–0 Trojans almost all the way back. They were even back in the Rose Bowl for the first time in five seasons.

That was the good news. The bad news? The No. 3 Duke Blue Devils of the great Wallace Wade would be the Trojans' opponent in Pasadena, and the team from Durham, North Carolina, had yet to yield a single point all season. It was the start of a trend, with Tennessee showing up the next year for the 1940 Rose Bowl, also having allowed zero points in a full season. But that would be a problem for next year.

USC All-American quarterback Grenville "Grenny" Lansdell carries the ball against Notre Dame in 1938.

The "Seven Iron Dukes" Blue Devils defensive front, responsible for the 9–0–0 record Duke brought to the January 2 game, were this year's problem. How do you lose when you refuse to let anyone score on you? They also had one of the nation's top backfield stars in halfback "Eric the Red" Tipton.

But having just defeated the nation's No. 1 team, the Trojans seemed to be up for the challenge of defending their four-game unbeaten Rose Bowl record, even without the kind of All-American cast that Jones's earlier USC teams featured. There was 5-foot-11, 218-pound guard Ernie Smith, in his first of two All-American seasons, out of Ontario.

Nicknamed "Blackjack," Smith changed the look of USC football with his athleticism and strength up front.

And from Pasadena came 197-pound do-everything quarterback Grenville "Grenny" Lansdell, USC's offensive leader who would find himself very much up against an unyielding Duke defense for more than three scoreless quarters. Duke then got a twenty-three-yard field goal in the fourth quarter to go ahead, 3–0, making it look like the East Coast team might actually complete a perfect season in which they'd allow no points.

But that's not why Steve Bisheff and Loel Schrader rank this as one of "The Ten Greatest Games" in USC football history in *Fight On!: the Colorful Story of USC Football*. What happened next is. As the authors describe it, USC was not going to be able to run the ball against that Duke front, but there was a fourth-string Trojan quarterback with "a rifle arm"—Doyle Nave. The 5-foot-11, 180-pound junior out of Los Angeles Manual Arts High had been waiting for this moment, they write.

Speedy receiver "Antelope" Al Krueger, a backup end who grew up in Antelope Valley, would also get his chance to shine, but not before it looked like USC had blown it.

With the clock running down, the Trojans took over with an opportunity to win after recovering a fumbled punt at the Duke ten. But three plays gained nothing, and a missed field goal had USC in big trouble. Fortunately for the Trojans, Duke couldn't move the ball either, punting to the USC thirty-nine. With two minutes left, USC was at the thirty-four but with no answer yet.

This is where the story gets murky. One tale, as documented in Bisheff and Schrader's account, has it that Jones's deep staff of assistants came through for him. Top assistant Sam Barry, along with Julie Bescos and Bob McNeish, wanted Nave in the game to throw the ball immediately. Nave would be the guy for the job, even if he'd played just twenty-eight-and-a-half minutes all year, not enough officially to earn a letter.

But the "real" story, according to an insider as told to the *Los Angeles Times* years later, appears to have been a little less straightforward. Apparently, USC assistant Joe Wilensky, who was taking the signals on the sideline from the coaches, knew that Barry wanted Nave in. But Barry hadn't asked him to tell Jones in so many words. So when he and the other assistants headed down from the press box to the field in the final minutes, Wilensky on his own told head coach Howard Jones, an imposing Hall of Fame figure, that Barry had said to put Nave in. It would have much more impact coming from Barry, Wilensky felt. Jones believed him and went ahead and put Nave in—and the rest is history. Yet the coaches didn't want to tell Jones of the subterfuge, so they kept it secret for a decade. At least that's the story!

With the message relayed to Jones, he sought out Nave on the bench. "I was sitting about three seats from Jones on the bench and he said to me, 'Doyle, I'm thinking about putting you in,'" Nave told the *LA Times* in 1988. "What have you got in mind?" he asked his head coach.

Jones replied, "The 27 series. Get the ball to Krueger. He's the best end we have for getting open."

So in Nave went, completing his first three passes from the thirty-four—one for thirteen yards, another for four, a third for a loss of two—all to Krueger. And then came the "27" series, with Nave telling Krueger: "I want you to go to the corner of the end zone. Do all the faking you want, because our guys are doing a great job of blocking."

Nave continued: "I faded back to the thirty-one- or thirty-two-yard line, and, as soon as Al made his move, I threw that damn thing as hard as I could right into the corner, and he was there."

In 598 minutes of football, Duke had not allowed a single point all season. And then in a minute and twenty seconds, the right arm of Doyle Nave would record for the Trojans the only seven points surrendered that year by Duke. And a 7–3 Rose Bowl win would announce to the world that Howard Jones's Herd was back. The Trojans would solidify their message with a second Rose Bowl win over another team from the South—Tennessee, which had also not given up a single point that season—a year later. USC would also claim a national championship that year.

But against Duke, this was about celebrating a win that looked out of reach for the Trojans until Doyle Nave arrived. And everything changed.

As it turned out, they didn't have to worry about time, covering the final thirty-four yards in four plays and the span of 1:20. Modern football had arrived at USC, the West Coast, and for the college game. Nave would become instantly famous, getting congratulations from all over the nation—but no game ball, as Bisheff and Schrader point out. USC had a rule: Only seniors get game balls.

So the next season, when Nave was a senior, in the first home game, he was awarded a game ball as well as a lifetime pass to USC home football games, something USC reserved for players who lettered all three varsity seasons.

For Nave's thirty minutes of play the year before, and his Rose Bowl heroics, he received a letter to go with his Co-MVP award from the Rose Bowl that he shared with Krueger, who would go on to play for the Washington Redskins. "I caught touchdown passes from Sammy Baugh when I was with the Redskins, but there was no one better than Doyle Nave, not even Baugh," Krueger would be quoted.

Nave, a first-round NFL draft pick by the Detroit Lions, would choose to bypass the NFL for a career as a motion picture cameraman. But first, like so many of the players of that era, Nave would head off to World War II and Navy duty as an officer on a carrier in the South Pacific. It was there that he would meet an officer on an adjoining carrier,

Dan Hill, the center on that Duke team. "I asked Dan whether he had any idea that I was going to pass when I came into the game," Nave told the *LA Times*. "He said, 'Hell, no. We didn't even know who you were.'"

But USC fans did—or at least now they do.

7

A championship delayed . . .
for sixty-five seasons

It took a while—sixty-five years, to be exact—before USC would claim its 1939 national championship trophy. But the opportunity had been there all along for Howard Jones's Trojans to nail No. 4 to the wall in Troy.

It took some serious research, though, before that unbeaten USC team (8–0–2) was declared the national champion.

"It was brought to our attention by various individuals that we should be claiming the 1939 Trojans among our national champions in football," USC Director of Athletics Mike Garrett told the *Washington Times* before the 2004 season opener at FedEx Field against Virginia Tech. "We took this matter seriously, did significant research, and determined this to be true. That 1939 team was one of the greatest in our history."

But in finishing an 11–0 season, Texas A&M—No. 1 in the AP voting before the bowl games—barely beat No. 5 Tulane, 14–13, in the Sugar Bowl. That left things open for USC's Trojans, who were playing the unbeaten Tennessee Vols (who had not been scored on all season), considered by some the No. 1 team in the nation.

Of course, none of this would have counted had USC not survived big-time regular-season challenges from the likes of No. 11 Oregon State (a 19–7 road win), Washington, Notre Dame, and UCLA.

Not that the Trojans survived completely unscathed. They opened with a tie—7–7 against Oregon—and closed with one—0–0 against No. 7 UCLA. This was the first time both teams had been ranked in the Top Ten going into their game (USC was No. 3 at the time). It was also the first time that the Rose Bowl was on the line, resulting in a Coliseum crowd of 103,303.

Two-time (1938,1939) All-American tackle Harry "Blackjack" Smith was a big part of Howard Jones's later Trojans teams.

The Trojans, with the better record and higher AP ranking, knew that a tie in the Crosstown Rivalry game would send them to the Rose Bowl. So tie is just what they did.

But the Trojans also had to win a regular season game by the skin of their teeth, 9–7 at home against Washington. This victory came the week after beating No. 7 Notre Dame, 20–12, in conditions classified in the *USC Media Guide* as "cold," for what would be the 400th game in Irish football history according to *The USC Trojans Football Encyclopedia*. Trailing by two, Notre Dame went for a first down on their own thirty-nine with four minutes left and missed. USC then scored on its second play on a thirty-nine-yard run by Ambrose Schindler to seal the deal.

Schindler, it must be noted, more than sixty years removed from his USC playing days at the age of eighty-seven, was one of the leaders who asked for USC to reconsider how that 1939 team's national championship had "fallen through the cracks."

"We were not asking for a new championship," the *Washington Times* quoted Schindler. "This is just a reinstituted championship that was taken away. The school acknowledged we were national champions back then. In our yearbook we were referred to as national champions across the top of the photo. Somewhere along the line, in the next 20 years or so, we were eliminated by the school as national champions.

"We didn't realize it until they started putting up banners denoting championship teams, and our team was not there," Schindler said. "We complained about it, but no one would listen, so we started collecting materials and presented the case to Mike Garrett, who saw the value of our claim."

Ultimately, those Trojans sealed the deal at the Rose Bowl, where Howard Jones had been a perfect 4–0 in his career. Perfect, however, was also the exact word to describe this Tennessee team on its way to Pasadena. General Robert Neyland's team had been riding high on a twenty-three-game win streak. Both teams were chasing another unbeaten team, Texas A&M, as they headed into the big bowl in the Arroyo Seco.

Led by tackle Harry "Blackjack" Smith (5-11, 218), a unanimous All-American born in Missouri by way of Ontario, California, and quarterback Granville "Granny" Lansdell (6-0, 187), a native of Great Barrington, Massachusetts, by way of Pasadena Community College, the Trojans beat the Vols and it wasn't all that close.

Smith, later inducted into the College Football Hall of Fame, would go on to play for the Detroit Lions, then coach at Missouri and USC, before becoming head coach of the Saskatchewan Roughriders in the CFL. At 218 pounds, Smith, who earned his "Blackjack" nickname for the way he hammered opponents, was just too strong for most college teams of the day to handle.

Listed as a quarterback, Lansdell was USC's leading passer for three straight seasons, its leading rusher for two, and its leading scorer for another as a classic do-everything single wing tailback-type player. He became the first junior college transfer at USC to earn All-American honors. He would go on to play for the New York Giants the final season before WW II and then go into the Air Force as a pilot. He would not return to football, finishing his professional career as a TWA captain for more than three decades.

Lansdell would rush for 51 yards and Schindler for another 81 as USC gained 229 yards on the ground against the previously impenetrable Vol defense in a 14–0 win that saw the Trojans score once in each half.

As it turned out, USC was bigger, stronger, and faster than Tennessee, not to mention the more experienced bowl team as they sent Howard Jones, who would die of a heart attack in the summer before the 1941 season, off with a perfect 5–0 Rose Bowl record.

After the season and that dominating win against Tennessee, USC was presented the Knute Rockne Trophy by Dr. Frank G. Dickinson, a University of Illinois economics professor whose mathematics-driven analysis would pick the national champions and rank college football teams from 1926 through 1940. He had the Trojans as the nation's No. 1

team. "The Trojans were the best team in the best section [of the nation]," Dickinson said. "And the nation's other top teams did not play as strong a schedule as USC."

Asked to rank the two teams—Texas A&M and USC—according to his twenty-first Century system, one of the BCS computer analysts, Richard Billingsley, said he figured it at 298 to 296 in ranking points. "They were very close," Billingsley was quoted. "USC beat Tennessee in the Rose Bowl pretty convincingly and Tennessee was ranked No.1 [by some] going into the game." So . . .

There would be no argument from Tennessee's Gen. Neyland: "We weren't off form, stale, or crippled," Neyland said, "we were just outclassed."

"This has nothing to do with other teams," USC Sports Information Director Tim Tessalone said of the late-breaking national title claim. "There is no one determining body to pick a champion, so it is really up to the individual schools. This whole thing is what makes college football so much fun."

8

That day C.R. Roberts integrated Texas—and Southwest Conference—football

USC football was not unaccustomed to traveling across the country to play powerhouse programs. The Trojans had inaugurated the most famous intersectional rivalry in college football history against Notre Dame in 1926. To this day, they've followed with trips to Boston and Miami, State College and Lincoln, Baton Rouge and Tallahassee, Little Rock and Columbus, Minnesota, New York, and D.C., among many other locations.

Anytime. Anywhere.

Most famously, the Trojans traveled to Birmingham at the height of the civil rights movement in 1970 for that long-remembered matchup with Alabama and Paul "Bear" Bryant that helped liberate Southeastern Conference football after a three-touchdown performance by Sam "Bam" Cunningham in a 42–21 USC romp.

But as important as that moment was, it wasn't a first for a USC program that had an African-American, Brice Taylor, as its first-ever All-American in 1925.

Then, more than thirty years later, the Trojans would hit town in a segregated Austin, Texas, in September 1956 for the season opener against the University of Texas Longhorns. And would do so with C.R. Roberts as their featured running back.

Roberts was used to being in the minority. He'd been one of just three African-American players on his Carlsbad-Oceanside High team. And at USC, the numbers hadn't changed. He may have been the president of his fraternity, but the 6-foot-3, 215-pound fullback was one of just three African-American players on a USC team headed for that season opener in pre-civil rights Austin—where the hotel and stadium were both segregated. Those three USC players would not be allowed to stay with their teammates, they were informed, according to the law there.

C.R. Roberts.

C.R. described the Texas trip on his own website. As recounted by Roberts, Coach Jess Hill threatened to cancel the game, before the black players were told they would be allowed to stay in a YMCA outside of the town. When Roberts refused, ultimately the team was permitted to stay at a hotel that Roberts believed was owned by a USC alum. Hill is reported to have said to the hotel management where they ultimately stayed that "We all stay here or none of us do," as reported in *Fight On!: the Colorful Story of USC Football.*

Despite the initial difficulties, Roberts wrote how incredible what happened during and after the game was: "As I warmed up, I could hear the loudest cheering coming from the end zone where the blacks and Mexican[-American]s were encouraged to see football in this stadium for the first time. And tonight, they were cheering for us, USC. . . . I remember that we played some good football that game, but I remember what happened after the game most of all." Roberts then explained how countless black hotel workers visited the team that evening, and how he and his roommate spent all night talking with their visitors. As they talked, he said he recognized the historical significance of the game, which marked the first time a DI team had played an integrated team in the Southwest Football Conference.

USC's first night game outside the state of California had the Trojans giving their built-in cheering section in the segregated end zone much to cheer about. For Roberts, it was an almost eerie foreshadowing of Cunningham's three-touchdown, twelve-carry performance fourteen years later in Birmingham—and one of those moments that can make a career.

It was certainly a moment that no Trojans running back in all previous years had ever come close to. Nor for the next twenty-three years afterward. In his twelve carries, Roberts ran for a USC-record 251 yards with touchdown runs of seventy-three yards, fifty yards, and seventy-four yards in just twelve minutes of action in USC's 44–20 romp over Texas. That's all it took. It was almost like being back in high school, when Roberts, the 1953 California High School Player of the Year, scored a San Diego County record 395 points.

Roberts certainly could have scored more against the Longhorns. "I was having a pretty good night," Roberts would tell the *San Diego Union-Tribune* in the understatement of a lifetime. But enough was enough.

"Coach [Hill] pulled me out because there was getting to be a lot of tension in the air," Roberts said. Nevertheless, as Roberts explained, "Just by getting to play in that game, I felt I had won."

Roberts's winning ways wouldn't stop on the football field. He would go on to add a master's degree in educational administration to his undergrad diploma in business administration from USC. He would also play four years in the NFL for the San Francisco 49ers in what was known as the "all-initial backfield" of Y.A. Tittle, R.C. Owens, J.D. Smith, and C.R. Roberts. He then put in another three seasons in the Canadian Football League.

Two things C.R. managed to accomplish during his time in student government at USC: he pushed for USC to allow female students to be able to join the all-male cheerleading squad and to integrate USC's fraternities and sororities for the first time.

Throughout his life, sports had never come first for C.R., not even at USC for this son of a Mississippi Delta farmer whose family moved to California when C.R. was in the third grade so his dad could work for the railroad. Roberts joked, "[you] know how people say somebody's from the wrong side of the tracks? We lived right *next* to the tracks."

While he could run and jump (in college, C.R. once beat UCLA's Rafer Johnson, the Olympic decathlon champ, with a long jump of 24-3), the thing he said he loved the most, the thing he had to give up because of football's time constraints in college, came elsewhere. "I was commander of the ROTC team. As a kid, I got to hang around with the Marines in town and at Camp Pendleton, and I knew everything about the military, all the weapons and all the vehicles. I wanted to be like them, the best of the best."

But his career choices after professional football would take him elsewhere. He would be named to President Ronald Reagan's Inner Circle and President Bill Clinton's Grass Roots Initiative. He also managed the transportation for athletes, coaches, media, and celebrities in the 1984 LA Olympics. C.R. would go on to a life focused in a number of directions—as an educational administrator and as a lay leader in the Methodist Church. He also owned a travel agency and served as vice-president of the Retired NFL Players Association for two years.

As far as that Texas game goes, in another interview, C.R. said, "There's no way to explain it really. I was focused, the team was fired up, the events surrounding the game worked in our favor instead of the other way, but Texas was good, there's no real explanation . . ."

Except for this: "I think actually being a Trojan is more special than any other group . . . being a Trojan is something special. We played ball but we do a lot of other things . . . when the team said they'd not play if I didn't play, that made me feel good, and we came together."

9

John McKay somehow survives first two years, wins it all in Year Three

College football looked like it had passed the USC Trojans by. It had been twenty-three years—the entire decades of the 1940s and 1950s—since USC had not gotten anywhere close to the glory of the Howard Jones Era, when it won four national titles in twelve seasons from 1928 to 1939. Sure, they'd had some great players—College Football Hall of Famers John Ferraro, Frank Gifford (who was also a Pro Football Hall of Famer), "Jaguar Jon" Arnett, and Mike McKeever and Pro Football Hall of Famer Ron Mix.

But there were just three Top Ten finishes in those twenty-three years and nothing higher than the No. 5 AP spot in 1952. Certainly nothing was happening in 1960 and 1961, the first two seasons for USC's new head coach, John McKay, just thirty-seven years old. A former Purdue and Oregon player, Oregon assistant coach, WWII Air Force veteran, and native of tiny Shinnston, West Virginia (population 3,000), McKay had used the combination of college football and the war to escape the coal mines of his native state.

A top high school athlete, McKay had been forced to start working at the age of thirteen due to the sudden death of his father, a mine superintendent. His ambition after college was to return to Shinnston—a town that would easily fit, he said, in the LA Memorial Coliseum, where his Trojans played—as the football-basketball coach.

But the war intervened, and McKay went from an athletics instructor to tail-gunner in the Pacific at the war's end before moving on to college, thanks to the GI Bill. Purdue came first, then a transfer to Oregon, the best move he ever made, he says, because it got him into college coaching after he received his degree and finished his playing career.

But it wasn't looking good for McKay at USC. He'd won a mere eight games (4–6–0 in 1960, 4–5–1 in 1961) and just escaped firing after his second season thanks to having upset a favored UCLA in 1960, the first time he faced the Bruins.

McKay would get one more chance—which, as it turned out, is all it would take. McKay could laugh at his predicament in this high-pressure world, with his famous "gallows humor" that helped him survive. "I'll never be hung in effigy," he said in his delightfully candid autobiography, *McKay: A Coach's Story* as told to Jim Perry. "Before every season, I send out my men to buy up all the rope in Los Angeles."

McKay did more than that by Year Three of his tenure. He'd recruited his kind of tough, physical, hard-nosed players, who opened with a 14–7 win over eighth-ranked Duke, earning a No. 9 ranking in the AP Polls for the Trojans the next week before they dispatched Southern Methodist (33–3). They subsequently took two trips in three weeks for wins in Big Ten country—7–0 at Iowa and 28–16 at Illinois—sandwiched around a 32–6 win over California. In their Week 6 Homecoming matchup, the No. 3 Trojans faced No. 9 Washington, whom they defeated, 14–0.

John McKay in a postgame presser with sportswriters including legendary *Los Angeles Times* sports columnist Jim Murray, far right.

That got USC up to No. 2, and wins over Stanford (39–14) and Navy (13–6) set up the big finish for the now-No. 1 Trojans against archrivals UCLA and Notre Dame.

There were stars everywhere. On offense, the nation's first-ever big-bodied All-American wide receiver, "Prince Hal" Bedsole, at 6-foot-5, 221 pounds, led the way. To this day he has the career mark in yards-per-pass reception (20.4). There were a pair of quarterbacks to get the ball to him, as Bill Nelsen and Pete Beathard combined for eighteen touchdown passes against just three interceptions. Tailback Willie Brown led USC in rushing, interceptions, punt returns, and kickoff returns and paired with 215-pound fullback Ben Wilson in a powerful ground attack.

Big and athletic at 6-foot-5 and 221 pounds, USC All-American wide receiver Hal Bedsole led the Trojans to a 42–37 national championship win in the 1963 Rose Bowl over Wisconsin.

A defense led by All-American linebacker Damon Bame and featuring tough guy tackle Marv Marinovich limited regular season opponents to 55 points, with UCLA scoring just three points during a win the week before Notre Dame's arrival. The result: Trojans 25, Irish 0. A No. 1 USC would advance to the Rose Bowl with a chance to win that elusive national championship against second-ranked Big Ten champions Wisconsin.

The nation's highest scoring team, Wisconsin, had beaten then-top-ranked Northwestern by thirty-one points and was a two-point favorite despite USC's No. 1 ranking. "The pressure, needless to say, was incredible," McKay said. "It hit me the first time I came out and saw over 100,000 people [official paid attendance 98,698] in the stands."

Let McKay tell you the story of how it went down after the completion of the first three quarters of the Rose Bowl. "I remember standing on the sideline that first day in January, 1963, basking in the glow of a 42–14 lead over Wisconsin. There were only twelve minutes left in the game and I was on my way to coaching USC to its first unbeaten, untied season in thirty years. A spectacular victory seemed inevitable," McKay said.

But, and you knew there would be a "*but*," Wisconsin scored quickly, making it 42–21. So McKay changed his approach from all-out attacking. "I decided to be conservative," he wrote.

So he gave Wilson a directive: "I put my arm around him, and said, 'Ben, go in there and tell the quarterback to run you up the middle three straight times. And Ben, for God's sake, don't fumble.' And on the first play, they hit old Ben and the ball popped out of his arms and rolled back to our 29. And Wisconsin recovered and Ben slumped off the field. 'Ben,' I screamed at him, I told you not to fumble. 'Coach,' he said, 'I didn't hear you.'"

That was the start of an incredible fourth-quarter Badgers' barrage that saw two more quick touchdowns, a safety, and one more near score in a game that would end up looking much more like a modern-day game than one that happened 55 years ago, as Wisconsin quarterback Ron Vander Kelen completed 18 of 22 passes in the fourth quarter alone in the most exciting and high-powered offensive Rose Bowl played in the twentieth century.

"My God, what a game it was," McKay wrote in his book, "it lasted only slightly less long than the War of 1812." USC won it, thanks to Beathard's record four touchdown passes including two to Bedsole—one for 23 yards, the other for 57. Although Wisconsin's comeback seemed to get much of the notice, McKay wasn't all that impressed.

"You would have thought we lost," McKay said of the criticism he was hearing leaving the field. "'Wisconsin,' I said it like a swear word," McKay recalled of his postgame talk to his team. "Our intention was to win today—and what does the scoreboard say?"

The college football scoreboard would say something else about the McKay Era from 1962 through 1981, when the Trojans won five national championships (four under McKay, one under his top assistant and successor John Robinson), played in 11 Rose Bowls, won four Heisman Trophies, and produced dozens of All-Americans.

Of course, it all started (officially anyway) that New Year's Day in 1963 when the Trojans returned to the top of the college football world and, for the most part, stayed there.

"The trouble with winning, however, is you never take the time to enjoy it," McKay said. "As soon as one game is over, you begin to worry about the next one. As soon as one season is over, the same thing happens. As soon as you win one national championship, you're not successful with the public unless you win another."

McKay would be successful—winning three more before leaving for the NFL. Only his close friend Paul "Bear" Bryant and now Nick Saban, with six each, have won more.

It all started for McKay in that 1963 Rose Bowl, a game that lasted, well, forever. *LA Times* sports columnist Jim Murray picked up on the theme: "It started in broad daylight but it ended up under conditions so dark a man would bump into an elephant. The official timer needed a calendar. If the game lasted one more quarter, they would have run into next year's Rose Parade traffic."

10

"Greatest game ever played" comes down to one play

It was just one run, one play, one carry for a guy USC coach John McKay never hesitated to call on to carry the ball as much as McKay needed him to.

"It's not heavy," McKay said when asked how many times he asked Hall of Famer and Heisman Trophy winner O.J. Simpson to carry the football. "And he's not in a union. He can carry the ball as much as we ask him to."

On November 18, 1967, there was only one run that mattered, though—one play as the fourth-ranked Trojans battled the No. 1 UCLA Bruins, led by their Heisman Trophy-winning quarterback Gary Beban, for what could well be deciding game for the national title in front of 90,772 fans at the Coliseum. USC was coming off its lone loss of the season, 3–0 to Oregon State, in a quagmire in rainy Corvallis despite Simpson's 188 yards rushing as he returned from a sprained foot. So this was do or die. With a tie, UCLA would advance to the Rose Bowl. So it was win or else for the Trojans.

That OSU loss had knocked the Trojans out of the top spot nationally, which they'd held for six weeks thanks to wins over Stanford (30–0), Notre Dame (24–7 for the first win in South Bend since 1939), Washington (23–6), Oregon (28–6), and California (31–12).

They'd already defeated No. 5 Texas (17–13) at home and Michigan State (21–17) on the road. But thanks to USC loss, the unbeaten Bruins (with one tie) jumped to the top spot, replacing the Trojans.

Much of USC's success had to do with the 6-foot-2, 210-pound Simpson with his 9.3-second speed in the 100-yard dash. He carried the ball an average twenty-nine times a game his junior year, his first at USC as a transfer from San Francisco City College. It

In his Heisman Trophy-winning 1968 season, O.J. Simpson carries the ball in a 35–17 win over No. 11 Cal.
Associated Press

seemed that the more he ran, the better it was for USC. As McKay wrote in *McKay: A Coach's Story*. "Simpson gets faster in the fourth quarter, and I get smarter."

On this day, with USC at its own thirty-six yard line on 3rd and 7 with under 11:00 left in the game and trailing 20–14, the Trojans clearly had to throw it . . . right?

But McKay had given his smart backup quarterback Toby Page the authority to change the play call at the line of scrimmage. And that is exactly what Page did, even though Simpson had told him he was tired and needed a rest—which was something he expected to get with a pass play called. But Page must not have heard—or believed—O.J.

As documented in *Fight On!*, when they got to the line of scrimmage and Page said he saw the UCLA linebacker moving outside to help cover one of USC's receivers, he called "red." He then changed the play to a "twenty-three blast," an O.J. run off left guard with the middle opened up. O.J.s reaction? "Toby, it's third and seven, this is a terrible call."

There are differing accounts regarding what happened next. UCLA linebacker, All-American Don Manning, has been quoted that he didn't move, he just missed the tackle on O.J. The USC guard supposed to make the block at the line of scrimmage, Steve Lehmer, said he didn't hear the play change call and apologized for not making the block. But it didn't matter. "O.J. just made a good move and I missed the tackle," Manning said. Simple as that.

Tired or not, O.J. was off on what would become for many people, including those responsible for the *USC Media Guide*, "the most famous run in college football history." Here's Page's description of the play: "O.J. went through Lehmer's hole, cut to the outside. I can still visualize O.J. running along the north sideline at the Coliseum and cut back to the middle about midfield. I knew then he was gone because the only guy fast enough to catch him was [Earl] McCullough and he was on our team. And he just kind of escorted him into the end zone."

"That's all she wrote," ABC-TV analyst Bud Wilkinson said. And it was in a game where, to that point, UCLA's 301 yards on Beban's passing had nearly doubled the 163 of USC—until O.J.'s run. "Sixty-four yards," his ABC partner Chris Schenkel added, "Sixty-four thrilling, captivating, collegiate football yards." Indeed.

Though in retrospect it appeared as if the play came somewhat easily, it was anything but that. As O.J. started inside, bursting smoothly through left guard, eight yards downfield, he had to hurdle a pile and head to the left sideline, almost tight-roping for a bit before smoothly reversing field. It was there that he put it into another gear, coming back across the field on a sixty-four-yard run that had him covering maybe twice that much distance before finishing in the end zone with 10:38 left in the game.

"An amazing athlete," McKay said of O.J. "Often he made yards entirely on his own—with everyone keying on him. . . . If you ever made a mistake on him, he was on his way to the end zone."

UCLA made the mistake and O.J. was on his way, much as he had been all season, like the day in South Bend when he led USC to its first win there since the 1939 season, 24–7 over Notre Dame. As Northwestern Coach Alex Agase said simply: "He approaches the hole like a panther and when he sees an opening, springs at the daylight."

Ultimately, USC would hold on for a 21–20 win over the Bruins that ABC televised nationally—one of just eight national TV games allowed that season. The game was covered by 200 reporters and 200 photographers, ABC's Chris Schenkel told the viewers,

All-American defensive end Tim Rossovich would help lead USC to the national title in 1967 and go on to a long career as an actor and Hollywood stunt man.

with ten TV cameras, an unheard of number in those days. And there was ABC's "Color slo-mo" camera, as well, which captured O.J. in all his glory.

Years later, ABC's Keith Jackson called it "the greatest game" he had ever seen. He received complete agreement from USC "Superfan" Giles Pellerin, who attended 797 straight games over seventy-two seasons for his alma mater. The game, with both Simpson and Beban, the Heisman winners in 1967 and 1968, earned the cover of *Sports Illustrated* for the pair, and the game was the big feature of that week's magazine.

"Whew! I'm glad I didn't go to the opera Saturday after all," wrote *LA Times* columnist Jim Murray. And yet the run—the second OJ TD run of the game—might not have been his best effort that day. He opened with a 13-yard TD on a sweep left that had seven UCLA defenders get a hand on him with OJ dragging the final two into the end zone. "Greatest run I ever saw," UCLA Coach Tommy Prothro said. "I didn't see any daylight," ABC's Wilkinson said, "but O.J. did."

Artist Arnold Friberg, commissioned by Chevrolet to do four paintings commemorating the first century of college football through 1969, chose to memorialize O.J.'s thirteen-yard TD, not the sixty-four-yarder, as Painting No. 4, calling it "O.J. Runs for Daylight." It would be featured in a national ad campaign for Chevrolet and then tour the nation's universities with the other three paintings.

Together, those O.J. plays ran the Trojans all the way to the Rose Bowl, where they faced sixth-ranked Indiana. A 14–3 win in Pasadena would give USC its second national title under McKay in six seasons.

But it wasn't all O.J. for USC's national title team. Tackle Ron Yary (6-5, 245) out of Bellflower was a consensus All-American, as well as USC's and the West Coast's first Outland Trophy winner, a member of both the College and Pro Football Halls of Fame, and a four-time Super Bowl participant. Consensus All-American linebacker Adrian Young (6-1, 210) from La Mirada set a Pac-12 record with four interceptions in USC's win at Notre Dame and would go on to play for the Eagles, Lions, and Bears. Consensus All-American defensive end Tim Rossovich (6-5, 235), out of Mountain View, would play for the Eagles, Chargers, and Oilers before going on to a movie career as a well-known actor and stunt man.

11

Sam "Bam" scores for and against Alabama and the Bear

The stage was set for history to be made. Two of the greatest coaches in college football history—John McKay and Paul "Bear" Bryant—were facing each other for a football game the night of September 9, 1970, in a still mostly segregated Birmingham, Alabama, in the still mostly segregated Southeastern Conference.

Thus it should come as no surprise how, after forty-eight years, the stories—the books, the documentaries, maybe even a movie—have multiplied and added to the legendary nature of that night even if the principals in that historic Trojans trip to Birmingham, Alabama, didn't recognize the historic nature of the event at that time.

"I never did pick up on it much," the hero of that game, Sam "Bam" Cunningham, says to this day. He talked about it on a trip back to Alabama with the 2003 USC football team as it opened at Auburn. "I'm from Santa Barbara," he would say with a laugh about the lovely California coastal enclave. Just a sophomore, he hadn't paid all that much attention to the bombings or the Bull Connor hosings of demonstrators demanding equal and fair treatment during those critical days earlier in the 1960s, when he and his USC teammates were still in grade school.

"We were just going there for a football game," Sam said as he reminisced more than three decades later. He didn't want to be remembered as any sort of civil rights hero. He was a football player. He says that although the majority of USC's fifteen black players felt pretty much the same as he did, some few were rumored to have acquired weapons to protect themselves if needed (which they weren't). Many of the players also realized something was different as their buses pulled up to Legion Field and hundreds of African-American

47

Paul "Bear" Bryant and John McKay, close friends and Hall of Fame coaches, set up one of the most important games in the history of college football when USC's integrated team traveled to Birmingham in 1970 to play a segregated Alabama team in the mostly segregated South as a signal that times—and college football—were changing.

fans lined the neighborhood streets waiting, watching, hoping, cheering, and praying for them. That was a wakeup call, Sam said. This was bigger than USC-Alabama.

Of course, no one knew that better than Bryant and McKay. Bryant had already recruited a black player, Wilbur Jackson, for the 1971 season and would get another, out-recruiting USC for a junior college transfer, John Mitchell, when Bryant learned the Trojans wanted him. Change was coming to the South and Alabama football. Bryant wanted to keep winning national championships, and without all the talent the state was producing, he knew he couldn't do that. This game would be a signal of what was coming.

USC's backfield of three African-Americans—fullback Cunningham, quarterback Jimmy Jones, and tailback Clarence Davis—didn't convince Bryant with USC's 42–21 whipping of the Crimson Tide. He already knew.

Yet the No. 3 Trojans were supposed to win. They were coming off a Rose Bowl victory over Michigan to end the 1969 season. Bryant's Alabama team was ranked No. 16 to start. What no one expected from the 6-foot-3, 212-pound Cunningham in his first start, and at fullback, where he'd spend much of his career as a terrific blocker for even more terrific tailbacks, was that McKay would give him the ball twelve times or that he'd pick up 135 yards and two times find himself hurdling into the Bama end zone—a living billboard for the talent that USC had and Bama needed.

Ultimately, USC was bigger, better, stronger, and won the way the Trojans should have. The almost entirely white Legion Field crowd of 72,175 sat mostly in silence as the inevitable played out—except of course for the small crowd of USC fans from Birmingham's African-American community in the end zone. But by the end of the game, USC's fans had increased tremendously as those neighbors who welcomed the USC buses gathered to send the Trojans off.

So did USC play the key role in integrating college football in the South, as the legend goes? Absolutely. Was this USC's doing? Probably not. It was coming. It had been decided. But USC was there to play an important part in making it happen on Bear Bryant's time line. To show how it had to happen. And that it could happen. And that is was really no big deal—just a football game between Alabama and Southern California.

Although there is this long-circulated quote from Bryant's top assistant Jerry Claiborne, who would go on to become a successful head coach at Virginia Tech and Kentucky: "Sam Cunningham did more to integrate Alabama in three hours than Martin Luther King had done in twenty years."

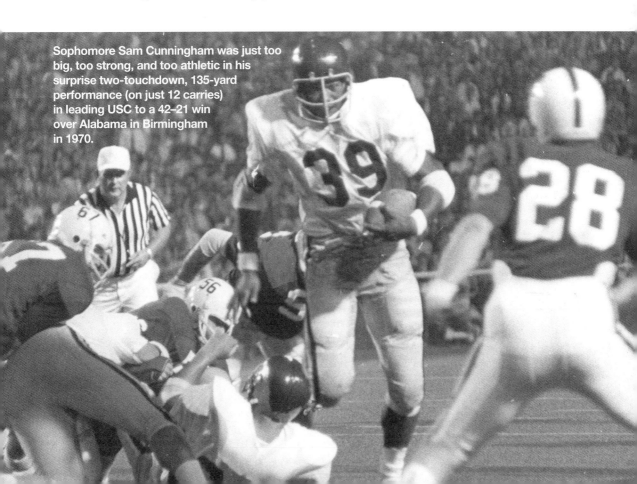

Sophomore Sam Cunningham was just too big, too strong, and too athletic in his surprise two-touchdown, 135-yard performance (on just 12 carries) in leading USC to a 42–21 win over Alabama in Birmingham in 1970.

As they always seem to have been, the Trojans would be involved in the integration of college football. It came as a result of John McKay's decision in the spring of 1969 to accept an invitation on behalf of USC to play at Alabama the following season. This came after the NCAA had increased the number of regular season games a team could play from ten to eleven. For McKay, getting a home-and-home against Alabama—and his buddy Bryant—made it even more attractive.

There's a terrific anecdote that comes via young assistant Craig Fertig, who served as McKay's chauffeur the day when the two coaches met secretly at LAX over drinks, as documented in Steven Travers's *Trojans Essential: Everything You Need to Know To Be a Real Fan!* As Fertig recalled, the two coaches had already agreed, for all intents and purposes, this was just to seal the deal, as Bear offered McKay $150,000 to bring USC to Alabama for the next season's opener.

"Bear's integratin' his program," Fertig immediately figured out where this was going, "Jesus, Mary and Joseph." A handshake sealed the deal, and that was pretty much it after McKay offered Alabama $250,000 to come to the Coliseum for the opener the following year.

But that was the future. This was about September 9, 1970. The only other national sports story that day came out of New York City, where the funeral of Vince Lombardi was held after the great NFL coach's much-too-early death at the age of fifty-seven.

College football that day was all about USC and Alabama, and no one better articulated what that meant than *Los Angeles Times* columnist Jim Murray in a piece titled HATRED SHUT OUT AS ALABAMA FINALLY JOINS THE UNION. He may have been writing for a mostly Los Angeles readership, but he knew who this game was about and where it mattered most—and it wasn't LA.

"The point of the game is not the score, the Bear, the Trojans; the point of the game will be reason, democracy, hope. The real winner will be Alabama."

Murray was more right than he could have guessed. While USC won that first Bama game big, in the short run, the Alabama games didn't do much for USC on the football field. The matchup in Birmingham outdrew the 67,781 who showed up the next year in LA for a game the newly, and barely integrated, Crimson Tide would win, 17–10, with their new triple-option offense. As for the 1970 and 1971 seasons, USC would struggle to a 6–4–1 mark in both with bowlless finishes.

But maybe for those sophomores like Cunningham, and fellow 1972 All-Americans Charles Young, Pete Adams, and John Grant, that Birmingham moment would stay with them in 1972 when that unbeaten Trojans team with that senior core of leaders would finish with a perfect 12–0 season and become one of the greatest teams in college football history.

But did Bryant really come over to the USC locker room and take Cunningham back over to his Bama players and say to them, "This here is what a college football player looks like," as the anecdote from that game has always contended? As often as it's been repeated, Bryant didn't have to. The folks in Alabama knew what a football player looked like. They knew what they'd seen. Though there appears to have been some kind of interaction between Cunningham and Bear, from all accounts it did not happen in the Bama locker room, and Sam himself says the postgame was such a blur, he can't say for sure what if anything specifically happened.

Nevertheless, this was about a football game. It didn't need to be about anything more—even if it was. And as so often seems to have happened in the history of college football, USC was there.

12

Greatest ever? 1972 Trojans will be in that discussion

There will be no end to this argument. No answer. No agreement. Not ever.

Which team was college football's greatest? Of course, there are lots of candidates—Notre Dame, Alabama, Oklahoma, Ohio State, and Miami would all have their nominees. But one thing is absolutely certain: John McKay's 1972 USC Trojans would be in the discussion.

Start with this staggering number. There were eleven players on that team who would be named All-American in their USC careers, including five from that 1972 season, when they finished 12–0–0 and never trailed in the second half of any game. Only fifteenth-ranked Stanford managed to come under double digits (in a 30–21 loss to USC), and the rest of the Trojans' ranked opponents did much worse.

No. 8 USC hit its stride in Week One when the team traveled to Little Rock to face the No. 4 Arkansas Razorbacks and drubbed the Southwest Conference team, 31–10, in a one-sided victory that propelled USC into the No. 1 spot they would not relinquish before being unanimously crowned the nation's No. 1 team by both the AP and UPI polls, something that had never happened until USC came along in 1972.

"Arkansas was talking national championship," McKay wrote in *McKay: A Coach's Story*, "but I thought we might surprise them."

After the game, Arkansas quarterback Joe Ferguson warned the rest of USC's opponents: "If USC doesn't go undefeated, then something's wrong," he said.

Three other ranked teams fell to the Trojans in the second half of the season—No. 18 Washington lost, 34–7, No. 14 UCLA was a 24–7 loser at the Coliseum, and finally No. 10 Notre Dame was a 45–23 loser in the season finale.

The 1972 USC national champion Trojans.

Next up for the 11–0–0 Trojans was the Rose Bowl against Big Ten champ Ohio State, the nation's No. 3 team and the toughest challenge all season for USC— on paper, anyway.

In front of a Rose Bowl-record crowd of 106,869 New Year's Day fans in Pasadena, it would prove less so—although it took the Trojans into the second half to make that clear. In fact, the game was tied 7–7 at halftime before fullback Sam "Bam" Cunningham leaped his way to a modern-day Rose Bowl-record four touchdowns and Player of the Game honors.

"Best blocking back I've ever seen," John McKay would say of Sam "Bam." "No defensive line was too high for Sam to dive over." That included Ohio State, which gave up repeated head-long leaps from no farther out than the two-yard line into the end zone.

But Sam was hardly alone. On offense, 1974 All-American tailback Anthony Davis (5-9, 183) out of San Fernando would rush for 157 yards, and quick, clutch starting quarterback Mike Rae, with Pat Haden behind him, would throw for 229 yards.

They were joined by unanimous All-American tight end Adrian "Tree" Young (6-4, 228) out of Fresno, who went on to play thirteen seasons in the NFL for the Eagles, Rams, 49ers, and Seahawks, including two Super Bowls, before being named to the Pac-12 All-Century Team in 2015.

Also on offense, San Diego's Pete Adams (6-4, 258) would go on to be a first-round pick for the Browns in 1973 as an offensive tackle and finish his career in Cleveland.

But this Trojans team was not all about offense. Explosive sophomore linebacker Richard Wood (6-2, 213) out of Elizabeth, New Jersey, arrived with a bang, becoming the first three-time Trojan first-team All-American whose inaugural game produced eighteen tackles against Arkansas and went on from there to anchor two USC national championship teams (also in 1974). USC's "Batman" would play a decade in the NFL and be inducted into the College Football Hall of Fame in 2007. His 4.5- second speed in the 40-yard dash allowed Wood "to run halfbacks down from behind," McKay said.

The All-American roster didn't end there. Boise, Idaho's, John Grant, a defensive end and tackle, would be named before moving on to seven seasons with the Denver Broncos. One of the smartest defenders he'd ever coached, McKay said of him.

By the numbers, this USC team averaged 39 points a game, scored 467 points—second most in school history—intercepted 28 passes, limited opponents to 2.5 yards a rush, and never allowed a run longer than 29 yards.

"It was a great team to coach," McKay was quoted in *Fight On: the Colorful Story of USC Football*. "They absolutely refused to make a mistake. We never had a down game." Of that nine-point win over Stanford as their closest call: "Only two college teams in the past 25 years did better than that," McKay noted.

USC would limit opponents to 132 yards of offense a game. "The perfect blend of talent, youth, and experience," the *USC Media Guide* describes that team.

It all came to reveal itself during the second half of that historic Rose Bowl against McKay's long-time coaching rival—Woody Hayes. It was a matchup made for the ages

USC 1967 All-Americans Adrian Young, center, and Tim Rossovich with Michigan State coach Duffy Daugherty at the Coaches All-American team unveiling.

and the first of three straight between the Trojans and the Buckeyes—two of which came with a national title on the line.

"This may be the best team Ohio State has ever played," Hayes told the *New York Times*, "and if we win we'll be entitled to the championship." McKay agreed: "This is the finest team I've coached," McKay said, better than his 1962 and 1967 national champions. Then he added, in his typical wise-cracking fashion, "There is no way we'll give back the MacArthur Bowl," which in those days was awarded to the national champion before the bowl games.

That 1972 Trojans team had 33 players who would eventually be drafted by NFL teams including five first-rounders—Young, Cunningham, Adams, and underclassmen Lynn Swann and Steve Riley. That Ohio State team had eight NFL first-rounders, including such stars as Archie Griffin, Doug France, John Hicks, and Randy Gradishar.

The *Los Angeles Times* led with this comment in that morning's preview of the Rose Bowl: "Well, the college football world can stop arguing about who will be No. 1 after today's game."

Indeed, they could. And no one could describe how that happened better than legendary *Sports Illustrated* college football columnist Dan Jenkins, who wrote: "When all the bowls were finally over, the question was not whether USC was still No. 1 but who might be No. 4, because surely these talented, flashy types of John McKay were No. 2 and No. 3 as well. Right? Next case."

USC didn't play like one of the greatest ever college football teams in a 7–7 first half. But they got things going after intermission as Anthony Davis got his game into gear for 157 yards rushing and quarterback Mike Rae got his arm in gear, as well, to finish with 229 passing yards in the game, much of those to tight end Young. And then of course, there was Cunningham's Rose Bowl record four-TD game as the Trojans' offense put up 35 points in the second half, outscoring the Buckeyes, 35–10.

"McKay simply had too many weapons for the Buckeyes," Jenkins wrote as the USC coach sent Davis to the bench to make way for Cunningham to finish his record-breaking day.

When all was said and done, McKay said, "I owe Sam something. He was a great runner, but I made him a blocker for three years. He's the best runner I ever ruined."

But no one ruined this 1972 USC team for the ages.

13

"The Comeback" . . . Nothing like it, before or since

It had happened once before in this legendary series, with these two Hall of Fame coaches, in this historic Coliseum. It happened with a stunned group of Trojans fans sitting there in silence as this rivalry game ending the regular season went from bad to worse.

The game was yet another example of a completely one-sided romp by the Irish against a USC team that had simply failed to show up. By the time it was over in 1966, Ara Parseghian's No. 1 Notre Dame was a 51–0 winner against John McKay's No. 10 Trojans. This time, in 1974, McKay's No. 5 Trojans—two seasons after a national championship run—were being taken to the woodshed once again by Ara's No. 6 Irish.

By the time the scoreboard reached 24–0 in favor of Notre Dame (with the nation's top defense) late in the first half, things were looking pretty bleak for USC. And then it happened. With ten seconds left in the half, USC's Anthony Davis got the Trojans on the board on a seven-yard pass from Pat Haden. But the Irish blocked the extra point, sending the Trojans into the locker room trailing, 24–6.

USC may not have been dead yet. But they weren't exactly breathing easily. There was no time to mess around, only time to get going—fast. And then it happened.

"THE COMEBACK."

That's all you have to say. It has its own special section in the *USC Media Guide*, with a photo of the scoreboard from late in the second half. On the top line, just as it was at halftime, there is Notre Dame, next to a point total of "24" (14 points in the first quarter, 10 in the second). But it's the bottom line that had changed, from "0" late in the first half to that lonely "6" at halftime to the final "55" at the very end.

That's right, USC scored 55 points in just under 17:00 against the nation's top defensive team. "We turned into madmen," is the way Davis described the turnaround he led from the second-half kickoff.

"I can't understand it," said wide receiver J.K. McKay, son of USC's head coach and one of leaders of that second-half rally, catching touchdown passes of 18 and 45 yards from his best friend, Haden. "I'm going to sit down tonight and have a beer and think about it. Against Notre Dame? Maybe Kent State . . . but Notre Dame?"

Yep, Notre Dame. In college football's most historic intersectional series ever in a one-of-a-kind game that will be remembered, well, forever. And it happened in an eye-blink, starting with Davis's 102-yard kickoff return touchdown when it looked like the Irish cover team must have blinked their eyes as Davis flew by. But that was just the kick-starter for the 35-point third quarter USC posted while shutting out Notre Dame.

Two more times Davis would finish off USC drives with short TD runs, and twice McKay would score on catches from his old high school buddy, Haden. And just like that, it was 41–24, USC.

But it wasn't over. In the first two minutes of the fourth quarter, Haden would hit Sheldon Diggs for a 16-yard touchdown and then immediately after that, Charles Phillips would score on a 58-yard interception. And there it was—55 points in 16:54—"THE COMEBACK" of all comebacks was in the books. USC 55, Notre Dame 24. Neither team would score again. The Trojans would be on to the Rose Bowl and a shot at another national title.

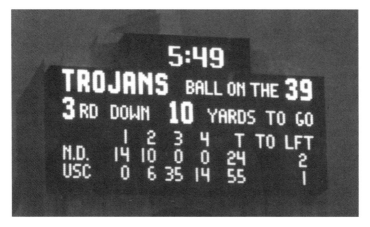

Fifty-five straight points in not quite 17 minutes is the unbelievable story this 1974 Coliseum scoreboard shows on that incredible "Comeback" day against Notre Dame.

But one question coming out of that game remains: why in the world would Notre Dame ever have kicked off to Anthony Davis, who had scored eight touchdowns in his

Anthony Davis on the run against Notre Dame. The Irish never could figure out a way to slow down the USC tailback.

previous two-and-a-half games against the Irish, including two kickoff return TDs in 1972? Parseghian said they didn't mean to, but that after the first kickoff attempt went out of bounds, the Notre Dame kicker got the ball just two yards deep into the end zone—deep, but not deep enough.

The avalanche had started. As top Notre Dame assistant Tom Pagna explained in *Fight On: The Colorful Story of USC Football*, "It was such an emotional shock. We were ahead by 24–0, but, you know, we've done things like that to other teams. We were never quite sure why or how it happened."

Though no one is quite sure why or how it occurred, according to USC fullback Dave Farmer, it started with a prediction from McKay: "A.D. is going to run the kickoff back for a touchdown," John McKay had told his Trojans team at halftime. Although when Davis heard him say it, he thought, "He's really crazy now.'" McKay said something else came out of that halftime talk with his team: "We agreed there was no NCAA rule against blocking."

But those wedge blockers—Ricky Bell, Mosi Tatupu, Bernard Tarver, and Farmer—clearly did not believe there was an NCAA rule against blocking on the kickoff, and all did so on Davis's touchdown run to start the second half.

As Farmer told Schrader and Bisheff, "I hit a guy off to my left, and Ricky hit a guy off to the right. And A.D. slithered through an opening and headed for the left sideline. He went all the way."

So good was this game for Davis, who would finish second to Archie Griffin in the Heisman Trophy voting, it changed the voting procedure. Ballots had been allowed to be submitted before the last games, which certainly cost Davis. Never again, the Heisman organizers said. Wait until all the regular season games have been played. "A lot of people credit me for changing the rules on the Heisman," Davis told the *LA Daily News*. "Most people think I won the Heisman."

So good was Davis against Notre Dame, with a six-touchdown game in USC's 45–23 1972 win, that Irish fans came up with a prayer for him the next year in South Bend: "Our Father who art in heaven, please don't let Anthony Davis get seven." He did, however, and it was on to 1974, when he would score four more.

So difficult was this game for Hall of Famer Parseghian to handle, many think it was the decisive factor in his coaching just once more in his college career. Although in so doing, he would do USC a great favor as Notre Dame upset No. 2 Alabama in the Orange Bowl, opening the way for USC, with a Rose Bowl win over No. 3 Ohio State, to contend for the national title. McKay wrote in 1974 in *McKay: a Coach's Story*: "The Fighting Irish were the first team in any sport I rooted for . . . today, I still cheer for them—except when they play us."

McKay had nothing but praise for Notre Dame, the campus, the Fight Song, Touchdown Jesus, the student body, the history, and the academics. The best moment in college football, he always said, was that October Saturday in South Bend when it was USC-Notre Dame time. Although in his best needling way, after one win over Notre Dame, McKay playfully jabbed at Notre Dame president Father Theodore Hesburgh that the loss was what Notre Dame got "for hiring a Presbyterian" like Parseghian. By the time of the 1974 game, USC, founded by Methodists but nondenominational, had more Catholic students than Notre Dame had. The Trojans also had an Irish Catholic coach.

But nothing motivated McKay as a coach like a loss, especially a tough loss. And that's what happened in 1966 in the Coliseum with No. 1 Notre Dame's 51–0 romp over the Trojans. After walking the first five miles home after the game with his son, as well as assistant Dave Levy, McKay vowed: "They'll never outtough us again. I think they won some of the early games that way, but they'll never do it again. They stuck it to us pretty good, and we ate a lot of humble pie."

But not on November 30, 1974, not after falling behind, 24–0. Not ever again. For *Sports Illustrated*, Joe Jares wrote, "That California Earthquake: It was caused by USC, it lasted almost seventeen minutes and its victim was Notre Dame. When it was over, Anthony Davis and his teammates were on solid ground while the Irish lay buried under a mountain of points."

14

A Trojan connection comes back to bite the Buckeyes

Looking back, Pat Haden, USC's Rhodes Scholar quarterback, had the perfect answer as to why the Rose Bowl was so special. As reported by Dan Sullivan on ESPN's *BCSfootball. com*: "In those days, the Rose Bowl had an ambiance and a reputation high above the other bowl games," Haden said. "It was the most special game on January 1, more than the Orange Bowl, more than the Sugar Bowl. It meant a lot to us at USC. If you grew up in Southern California watching the game, like I did, you wanted to participate in it."

Yet the 1975 Rose Bowl would be no easy feat, as once again the Trojans would match up against Ohio State, with a crowd of 106,721 looking on.

Ohio State's Heisman-winning Archie Griffin had his own ideas as to why the Rose Bowl was so special. As he told NBC, "It's why you work so hard in July and August and all season—to get here."

But as improbable as USC's comeback against Notre Dame might have been, that was not the end of the improbable happenings for this season—and for a USC team ranked no higher than No. 4 going into New Year's Day, when every single thing that could go its way did.

Starting with beating an Ohio State team ranked No. 2. That was a must. And USC had control of that, even if it trailed Ohio State by seven points with just over two minutes left in the Rose Bowl. But it had no control of how that Notre Dame team, after that comeback loss, would go on to the Orange Bowl and upset No. 1 Alabama.

But on top of that, there was an Oklahoma team, No. 1 in the AP Poll but on NCAA probation and forbidden to play in a bowl game and not eligible for the Coaches Poll, that was also out of the way. Win the Rose Bowl, and USC would have a shot to win half of the national championship.

So did the luck of the Irish rub off on the McKays, father and son, and honorary family member, quarterback Pat Haden, to have all that happen? It did.

But it didn't hurt that that USC team had 5 first-team All-Americans for the third straight year, a school-record 12 All-Conference players, and an all-time record 14 players—later tied by the 1976 team—who would be selected in the NFL draft. The Trojans also had the Heisman runner-up in senior tailback Anthony Davis, who, had they waited to vote until after Anthony's 4-touchdown performance in the season finale against Notre Dame, may well have won it. Anthony certainly believed he would after a season during which he rushed for 1,421 yards and scored 13 touchdowns.

All this didn't seem to translate to success on the field during the Rose Bowl, though, at least initially, as USC found itself trailing, 17–10, against an Ohio State team led by tailback Griffin, in the first of his unprecedented back-to-back Heisman-winning seasons.

High-stepping into the end zone was Anthony Davis's USC game. Here he does it against Ohio State in the Rose Bowl.

They could thank the USC defense, led by the Trojans' only three-time All-American to that time, linebacker Richard Wood, for keeping the Buckeyes relatively in check as USC doubled their yardage the first three quarters but couldn't cash in on the scoreboard. Wood had a great deal of help on a defense that forced the second-most interceptions in NCAA history, led by secondary star Charles Phillips, who set four NCAA interception records.

The Trojans needed to keep Ohio State close in this game. But a late fumble gave Ohio State an easy 34-yard field goal to make it 17–10. USC had the ball 84 yards away with less than 5:00 to go and its All-American tailback out with a second-quarter rib injury.

Then with 2:03 left, Haden would hit his buddy McKay on a perfectly on-target 38-yard scoring strike behind solid protection that brought the Trojans within one, 17–16. This forced John McKay to make a decision, much as he did trailing by a point against Purdue in the 1967 Rose Bowl, when he went for two and failed. Would he do it again?

"McKay's always been a gambler," Curt Gowdy said on the NBC telecast before his partner, Al DeRogatis, chimed in that "It takes character to go for two points here"—not to mention for the Rose Bowl and a possible national title.

After a long conversation on the sideline with assistant John Robinson and Haden, they had their answer: they would put the ball in Haden's hands to win or lose.

"We always go for two points in a situation like that," McKay was quoted in the *New York Times* after the game. "We didn't come to play for a tie, we were a fortunate team to win. They were unfortunate to lose."

That is just how it happened after Haden rolled quickly right, then stopped, elevated, and fired a low dart from a quick leap to a diving Shelton Diggs in the back of the end zone for the Trojans' game-winning two points when McKay was covered.

"That's my little claim to fame, that catch right there," Diggs told the *Los Angeles Times* looking back years later. "I didn't think about it then, and I don't think about it a lot now, but it's nice to know I did something to help USC win a national championship."

Woody Hayes was gracious in defeat. We got beaten by a better team," he said, "one point better."

"For me, it was a great moment," Haden said. "I didn't think I was going to be playing professionally, so I thought it was the last football game I was going to play. And to be able to throw the winning touchdown to your lifelong friend—that was thrilling."

The 10–1–1 Trojans would earn the 51-year-old McKay his fourth and final national title in his final Rose Bowl. Davis would make up for his Rose Bowl injury miss by following his 1973 NCAA championship baseball stint with the Trojans as an outfielder with another NCAA title in 1974.

USC won two national titles, with 1974 All-American defender Charles Phillips setting a number of NCAA and Pac-12 career interception records.

Along the way, they stopped Griffin's 22-game streak of gaining more than one hundred yards rushing, holding him to 76 yards and forcing fumbles on the USC 5- and 7-yard lines. USC tallied 24 first downs to the Buckeyes' fourteen and outgained them 463 yards to 286 in a crazy game where 8 turnovers did much of the stopping.

And as he usually did, John McKay had the last word: "There were 106,000 people in the stands, and no one knew who would win right up until the end. I thought it was a great game between two great teams, and in the end we had 18 points and they had 17."

15

When a win is forgotten and a national championship is split

John Robinson, the new sheriff in Troy, was picking up serious momentum—and talent— in his third season after taking over for his old boss, John McKay, after McKay had moved on to Tampa Bay in the NFL.

"Tailback U" had tailbacks everywhere you looked. Charles White was on his way to setting the Pac-12 career rushing record in his third season, and waiting in the wings as a freshman was one Marcus Allen. In his first two seasons, Robinson's teams had won 19 games, had finished second in 1976 with closing wins over UCLA, Notre Dame, and Michigan in the Rose Bowl, had finished twelfth the next season, and were starting 1978 as a solid No. 8.

Flash-forward to the third week of the season, and the Trojans, having moved up to No. 7, were on their way once again—for the first time since 1970—to Birmingham to play a now fully integrated Crimson Tide, the No. 1 team in the nation. Just a year before, the roles and the location had been reversed. Bear Bryant had brought his No. 7 Alabama team to the Coliseum to face the No. 1 Trojans and left with a 21–20 win as the Trojans went for two and failed with :35 remaining after scoring what could have been the game-winning touchdown.

But this was different. USC had Charlie White carrying the ball for the Trojans, and there wasn't all that much Alabama could do about him. Which is why, despite finishing the regular season with wins over No. 14 UCLA (27–25), No. 8 Notre Dame (17–10), and No. 5 Michigan (17–10) in the Rose Bowl, it's the Alabama game that people remember. That was the moment.

USC coach John Robinson congratulates his guys on the sideline.

As The Bear said simply, after watching the 6-foot, 185-pound White run for 199 yards in front of a sold-out crowd of 77,313 at Legion Field in leading USC to a 24–14 win: "I don't remember ever playing against a tailback who can run like White."

Not many had.

The two-time unanimous All-American and 1978 Heisman Trophy winner, USC's third, would go on to become, counting bowl games, the Pac-12's all-time leading rusher with 6,245 yards on an incredible 1,147 carries. Workhorse doesn't begin to describe White's four-year career. So why would that Alabama game have been any different?

Actually, the only folks who didn't seem to remember that game were the media members voting in the Associated Press poll, who refused to elevate the Trojans to No. 1. Beating No. 1 Alabama by ten points in Birmingham didn't do it. Defeating UCLA, Notre Dame, and Michigan to finish strong didn't do it. The AP voters stuck with the Tide, producing a split national champion in 1978, with the UPI Coaches Poll naming the Trojans their national champs and the AP going for the Crimson Tide despite the head-to-head loss to the Trojans.

The independent *tiptop25.com* website, which has documented college football polls throughout the years, calls the vote "the single worst AP Poll ever—excepting when they didn't count bowl games."

There was more, much more, from the *tiptop25.com* folks on that vote: "The only possible way Alabama could merit No.1 in 1978 after losing to Southern Cal by more than a touchdown at home is if Alabama played a markedly stronger schedule and/or outperformed USC by a country mile," they argue.

Schedule-wise, USC looked better against Alabama than it did that September day in 1978. In fact, *tiptop25.com* argued that USC played "one of the toughest [schedules] ever played by a national championship contender."

Although it really shouldn't have ever come to this. September 23 in Birmingham should have been enough. Sure, Alabama partisans say the Tide's defeat of top-ranked Penn State in the Sugar Bowl was enough to give the voters amnesia. And apparently it did. Furthermore, had USC not stubbed its toe badly in the desert, losing 20–7 to Arizona State, there would have been no argument. But as the *tiptop25.com* folks point out, Alabama's much easier schedule—a forerunner of the way things are played today—didn't offer many toe-stubbing possibilities. Alabama had just two close wins (a touchdown or less), the Bama partisans note, to USC's five, but that's discounted by USC's schedule that included nine Top 25 teams compared to Bama's five. This is coupled with the fact that the Trojans played six road games, compared to three by Alabama.

Despite all that, the Trojans got two very favorable calls, so in some ways luck may have been on their side after all. Against Notre Dame, a loose ball at the end was ruled an incomplete pass, giving USC the chance for a game-ending long completion and field goal to win, 27–25. And in the Rose Bowl against Michigan, a three-yard White touchdown plunge will always be disputed.

But back to Birmingham and that clash between the teams that would share national titles for 1978, here's how *Sports Illustrated's* John Underwood reported it in a piece headlined: IT WAS A SUM GAME, where he credited a 3.7 accounting major, USC quarterback Paul McDonald, for doing as much with his audibles, two passing touchdowns, and mistake-free ball-handling as White did in his 199-yard rushing effort, the most ever allowed by an Alabama defense.

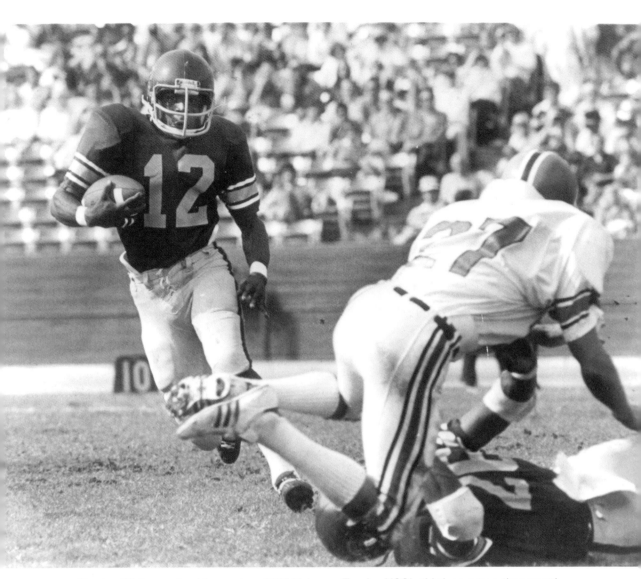

Charles White running his way to a 1979 Heisman Trophy, USC's third, as a two-time unanimous All-American tailback.

Sure, USC had all the stars it always has, Underwood said. It had speed and defense and toughness and all the things fans were starting to expect of the Trojans, but the smart decisions of USC's McDonald were the difference in a mistake-free road performance in Birmingham between two teams who would finish the season ranked No. 1.

Despite coming in as unbeaten 11-point underdogs with 14 players on the two-deep, including special teams players who had never played in a college game before, that USC team, featuring the kinds of sophisticated multiple shifts and motion that would make the Dallas Cowboys proud, would pile up 417 yards of offense against a defense some thought could have been Bryant's best.

White started it all with a 40-yard scoring run that included one high hurdle leap for good measure. "I'm faster than they think," White would say later. USC would also "match Bama BTU for BTU," as Underwood described it, bringing eight giant air-conditioning units to cool the sidelines at the Legion Field September sweat box.

Despite USC's relative youth, the Trojans' talent level was obvious. "I'd take their culls," Bryant said after the game. He wasn't far off. Thirteen players on that USC team would go on to play in the NFL: White, Allen, and McDonald, as well as Ronnie Lott, Anthony Munoz, Brad Budde, Riki Gray [Ellison], Brad Banks, Gary Cobb, Rich Dimler, Larry Braziel, Ray Butler, and Steve Busick.

Underwood credited USC for this list of Alabama failings: two fumbles, missed tackles and blocking assignments, four interceptions, backs running into one another, and "insatiable" USC special teams coverage.

Sports Illustrated described the scene in the dressing room after the game, as John Robinson hopped up onto a chair and addressed his team: "Remember what I told you Thursday . . . We're not No. 1, and I'm not voting us No. 1. I'm voting us No. 6. But you're the greatest bunch of human beings I've ever been around, and you're going to be a great team. I sense it. I feel it. You're not No. 1 now, but in January. . . "

Indeed, in January they were, except in the minds of those voters who forgot September.

Lefty All-American quarterback Paul McDonald slinging it against Notre Dame.

16

Marcus Allen: from fullback to tailback to "magnificent"

Marcus Allen's self-defined "miracle moment" may perhaps come as a surprise to people. As he made his way to becoming the player college football experts contend could do more things better than anybody who has ever played the game whether it was running the ball, catching the ball, or blocking for anybody else who had it—there were certainly a lot of highlights. In fact, Allen could even throw the ball. The guy could seemingly do it all.

The miracle moment did not come against Washington as a senior in the Seattle rain when he became the first college running back to exceed the 2,000-yard mark rushing in a single season, Marcus says. Nor was it the moment when he won the Heisman Trophy in a 1981 race so one-sided they really didn't need to count the votes.

Nor did it happen as an eleven-year-old in San Diego who was first pursuing football or when he moved on to Lincoln High School as a star running quarterback and safety in a prep career during which he also starred in basketball and baseball.

By the time he was a junior, Marcus Allen got to run the ball as a tailback after starting out as a fullback blocking for the tailbacks.

It didn't happen when USC coach John Robinson ran him out as an undersized sophomore fullback at 190 pounds to block for another Heisman Trophy-winning Trojan tailback, Charles White. "You're too good a football player not to have on the field," Marcus remembers Robinson telling him when he switched him from safety to fullback. "I thought I was going to be hitting people and here I was, blocking them and running into much bigger guys every day."

So the first-year varsity starter who had secretly dreamed of becoming O.J. Simpson one day, even if he didn't tell anybody, found himself asking the question "What have I gotten myself into?" as he threw his body play after play into defenders 40, 50, 60 pounds heavier than he, clearing the way for White.

But then White would graduate, and from a stable of top athletes at tailback, Robinson picked Marcus as the man up next.

"This is the toughest place to learn how to play tailback," he said of stepping into the position where Heisman winners Mike Garrett, Simpson, and White had been. "It was a tremendous amount of pressure to be that guy at USC. And then I was that guy."

Even during his junior year, when Marcus gained 1,563 yards on 354 carries—a tremendous workload for anyone, anywhere—it often didn't seem good enough. Marcus heard the critics, who'd complain that he'd slip on his cuts or that he'd try to bull through places where he shouldn't.

"People were questioning whether I was the right guy at tailback," he said. "What people didn't realize was that was my first year of running the ball. And I'll admit, I didn't really know what I was doing or understand the position. I was learning. Watching Charlie White helped, he was so tough and relentless. I put a lot into that first year. And I learned a lot."

So when spring football came around, and Marcus was heading into his senior season as a 6-foot-2, 210-pounder, he thought he was ready. Check that, he *knew* he was ready. "I'd gained 1,500 yards and didn't know what I was doing. And then I did. I was like a sponge. I tried to learn everything. By the middle of spring practice, I was confident. I knew the defenses. I knew the offense completely. I knew what everybody was going to do on every play. I knew I was mentally strong. I knew I was physically strong. I was able to play free."

According to Allen, that is precisely when the miracle moment finally came—in the spring. Not in a big game. Not with the crowd cheering. Not with the band playing "Fight On" as the Song Girls were doing their pom-pom thing. No, it came when his running backs coach, John Jackson, sat down with Marcus to go over his senior goals.

"He asked me what I wanted to do," Marcus recalls. "When I told him I planned to rush for 2,000 yards, to be the first running back to go over 2,000, he said, 'Marcus, be serious.' I told him, 'I am serious, Coach.'" In fact, he was even more serious than that, though he didn't tell his coach. "I was going to win the Heisman, too," Marcus says with a laugh. But he kept that to himself.

"That was my miracle moment—in spring football. At practice," Marcus says. "Games are a manifestation of what you do at practice. I had everything figured out. That was the miracle moment for me . . . the great games I had were a direct result of the way I practiced."

The great games came right away. Against Tennessee in the opener, Marcus racked up 210 yards on 22 carries followed by 274 on 40 carries against Indiana. Yet against Oklahoma in Game Three, when he carried the ball 39 times for 208 yards in a 28–24 USC victory, it became clear that he was the real deal.

By the time he was a senior, Marcus Allen broke the NCAA's 2000-yard barrier as the first college back to pass that mark in his Heisman Trophy-winning season.

The resilient Allen would carry the ball as many as 46 times a game. And he just kept rolling, getting his 200-yard-plus games to 8. He was not always taking people head on, although as his fullback blocking days showed, he could.

"Clearly we were a little bit in awe of what he was doing," Robinson is quoted as saying in Bisheff and Schrader's *Fight On!*. "He was such a great competitor. He was absolutely the best mental competitor I'd ever seen. He was smart and always knew how to get extra stuff out of any situation he was in."

By the time he was finished, Marcus had set or tied 16 NCAA records and had gained 2,342 yards—when no one else had ever reached 2,000. He led the NCAA in yards per game (212.5) and total yards per game (232.6) as well as scoring average (12.5 points a game).

He also led USC in receiving in 1980 and 1981 with a total of sixty-four catches. And he earned 441 first-place Heisman votes to runner-up Herschel Walker's 152 (totaling 1,797 points to Walker's 1,199), third-place Jim McMahon's 91, and Dan Marino's 16.

The honors would just be starting. Marcus earned the Maxwell and Walter Camp Awards as college football's top player in 1981.

He would be named to the College Football Hall of Fame and the Pro Football Hall of Fame after his 16-year NFL career and MVP Super Bowl selection.

"He was the greatest player I have ever seen," Robinson said.

Going into his senior season, Marcus knew he had a chance to be in that discussion.

"I wasn't confident, I was cocky," Marcus said, "because of the work I did."

As Washington State Coach Jim Walden said of Marcus, as quoted in Bisheff and Schrader's *Fight On!:* "He played Superman. I swear I saw him changing clothes in the phone booth. I even saw him fly over the stadium."

For a guy who could do it all with a football, maybe Marcus could, in fact, fly. After all, that wouldn't be much crazier than some of the other things he did.

17

Carson Palmer announces Carroll Era arrival against the Irish

It was coming. Clearly.

Pete Carroll's first USC team may have stumbled a bit out of the gate. But the 2001 Trojans were in every game, losing by just four, two, five, and three points in the first half of Pete's first season, and they might have defeated Notre Dame on the road had it not been for a screwed-up fake punt. They did rally, though, to ruin No. 20 UCLA's season in the 2001 finale for a four-game winning streak to get to a bowl after opening 1–4.

For a USC beat reporter hired on a July morning in 2002 to cover the Trojans, the plan that day was to head to campus and see if they were doing a players-only workout. They were—Troy Polamalu led the defense and Carson Palmer put the offense through its paces. It soon became clear that day that USC just might be back.

How far away could they be with just those guys in charge? Then there was this at the first scrimmage: a 6-foot-5, 225-pound freshman wide receiver from Florida named Mike Williams was simply undefendable. Too athletic. Didn't look like he'd just arrived in college.

Hold on, the critics said. USC will screw this up somehow. They always seem to. After all, this is a program without a national championship in twenty-four years, with only a couple of Top Ten finishes in that time, five head coaches (counting John Robinson twice), three losing seasons, and three more .500 seasons.

Gone were Robinson, Ted Tollner, Larry Smith, and Paul Hackett. Proud USC parent Pete Carroll, after a year of rethinking his approach after his NFL career with the Patriots and Jets hadn't gone exactly as he'd hoped, recruited AD Mike Garrett after USC had struck out on the school's first three choices. Sometimes, as USC learned, it's better to be lucky.

But better to be better, a lot better in 2002. There was no easy path to the top. USC opened with a 24–17 home win against Auburn (those were the days when the SEC traveled) in the opener, then a 40–3 romp at No. 18 Colorado. The Trojans were on their way until their third game, against No. 25 Kansas State on a second trip to the Big 8, caught up with the Trojans on a windy night in Manhattan, 27–20. No. 23 Oregon State was a 22–0 loser, and then came a fourth straight ranked opponent, No. 17 Washington State in Pullman, and a crazy 30–27 overtime loss that looked like it would knock the 3–2 Trojans out of the Rose Bowl in the early going.

The next week, the Trojans fell behind an unranked Cal, 21–3, before rallying for a 30–28 win. Ranked Pac-10 teams Washington and Oregon were next.

USC dispatched the No. 22 Huskies, 41–21, then went to Eugene and rolled on offense, 44–33, scoring 30 unanswered points in the second half in front of the largest crowd ever to watch a football game in Oregon to down the No. 14 Ducks. USC's quarterback was starting to look like something really special as the No. 15 Trojans worked their way into the Top Ten with one-sided romps over Stanford (49–17), Arizona State (34–13), and UCLA (52–21), reaching No. 6 as they welcomed a No. 7 Notre Dame to the Coliseum for the regular season finale.

This would be the moment that mattered. Beat Notre Dame, and USC still could not edge out Washington State for the Rose Bowl. But finish in the top four nationally, and that would qualify USC for a BCS berth and a January 1 bowl. A lot was on the line, as it so often has been in this series. It was do or die time for the Trojans' comeback season.

The Trojans went out a winner, shredding the Irish defense for 425 yards and four touchdowns passing as USC racked up 610 yards of offense against the nation's fifth-best defense to the delight of 91,432 fans (or at least most of them) in a 44–13 walkover at the Coliseum. No opposing team or player in all the seasons since the Irish first played football in 1887 had ever done better against Notre Dame. And the nation was watching as the Trojans earned their bid to face Big Ten cochamp Iowa in the Orange Bowl.

But it was—as is so often the case—the Notre Dame game that mattered most in 2002. It did for the Heisman Trophy voters, at least. No West Coast player had won the Heisman since USC's Marcus Allen in 1981. After all, Carson Palmer, a player the USC publicity operation barely campaigned for until season's end, was on no one's Heisman list until maybe the Oregon game in late October.

"He's got my [Heisman] vote," Notre Dame safety Gerome Sapp told *Sports Illustrated*'s Austin Murphy.

Carson Palmer survived injuries and all sorts of coaching changes to emerge from USC with a Heisman Trophy and became the No. 1 overall pick in the NFL Draft.

"If it happens, I'll be honored," Palmer said. "If it doesn't, I totally understand because there are a ton of great players out there, a ton of great guys."

But after the Notre Dame game, the media had no choice, as Palmer became USC's fifth Heisman Trophy winner and first-ever quarterback. So impressive was Palmer in those final two rivalry games that he won every voting region in the nation.

More important, it was USC's first sweep of UCLA and Notre Dame since 1981. The 62-point margin (31 in each game) was the most ever for USC in a rivalry sweep. Not a bad finish. Furthermore, the Trojans' No. 1 defense in the nation throttled the Irish, holding them to zero first downs in thirteen third-down conversion attempts.

Even as a freshman, big Mike Williams was a man against boys
wide receiver for the Trojans' turnaround under Pete Carroll.

"I hope everyone was paying attention and saw the score," Palmer said after exiting the
field waving the Jeweled Shillelagh, the game's traditional trophy. "They need to know that
we're for real now. We are definitely worthy of being a BCS team." Indeed. The Trojans
were rolling, with Williams grabbing ten passes for 169 yards and Justin Fargas running
for 120 yards.

In fact, the Trojans were rolling so fast that they went on a 45–1 tear, starting after
that Washington State loss and ending with the Texas Rose Bowl game after the 2005
season, when the only slip-up for the Trojans was the 34–31 three-overtime loss at Cal in

2003 as Pete Carroll kept things going with a whole new group of Trojans stars succeeding All-Americans Palmer, Polamalu, and Williams.

One of those wins would come in the Orange Bowl, where the Trojans were just too big, strong, athletic, and skilled for Iowa despite a slow start and the loss of Polamalu, who was recovering from a bad reaction to a shot for a hamstring injury. The 38–17 final ended the Hawkeyes' nine-game win streak and saw USC grind out 247 yards on the ground against an Iowa team ranked No. 2 in the nation in rushing defense. MVP Palmer played like a Heisman winner, hitting on 21 of 31 passes for 303 yards.

"It proved we're a heck of a team," Carroll said. "I couldn't imagine why somebody wouldn't want us to play in their game, although I know that some people might not want to play us."

The Orange Bowl, not to mention Notre Dame and Iowa, would agree.

18

Trojans' move back to the top starts at the other Alabama school

An upward-bound USC program had just said good-bye to the likes of Heisman Trophy winner Carson Palmer and All-American Troy Polamalu as well as top running back Justin Fargas, the backbone of the turnaround 2002 Orange Bowl-winning season that saw the Trojans finish No. 4 in the nation.

Yet coach Pete Carroll wasn't going to let the Trojans wallow. This is where one of Carroll's favorite principles kicked in: *"No whining, no complaining, no excuses."* No saying, "Woe is me, whatever shall we do?"

USC would do the one thing Carroll preached relentlessly: it would compete. The central principle of Pete's program said it best: "Competition is everything." But there were more, many more. One other such maxim of Carroll's that happens to be a favorite: *"Tradition Never Graduates."*

That held true in 2003, despite the departure of seniors Palmer, Polamalu, and Fargas. So what were the Trojans, No. 4 in the nation and maybe better than anyone else by the end of the 2002 season, going to do about it?

Well, for starters, they were going on the road, to a No. 6 Auburn team looking for revenge, the very next game to open the 2003 season. They did so with an untested quarterback, Matt Leinart, trusted with maybe half of offensive coordinator Norm Chow's playbook that day.

The game, which pitted the Trojans against an Auburn team with NFL talent all through the roster that some were picking to win it all, was arguably as important a game as any in modern USC football history. It set the tone for what was to come. This USC

Pete Carroll had good reason to smile, given the way his 2003 team started off on its national championship run—with a 23–0 road shutout of Auburn.

team would not be deterred by a wild, loud crowd of 86,063 screaming "War Eagle" up until halftime. The second half was pretty quiet.

This USC team may have been a bit on the young side, but nobody was pushing them around, not in the SEC, not in Alabama, not anywhere, and not anybody.

USC would beat Auburn 23–0 that day, and it wasn't as close as that 23-point differential suggests. Auburn got the ball across the 50-yard line once. It was the worst opening day loss in Tigers history.

It was also a tribute to how prophetic Auburn coach Tommy Tuberville could be. As the story goes, Tuberville would always stop by an orange-and-blue bus a block from Jordan-Hare Stadium every Friday before a game to chat with a longtime Auburn fan, who just happened to be talking to an LA reporter covering the Trojans.

"I don't think we can get up to the speed they're going to play with on defense," Tommy said of USC prior to the matchup. No truer words had ever been spoken. That USC defense forced ten Auburn punts and gave up just 43 yards rushing in 36 attempts. With 121 yards passing, that's a total offense of 164 yards for a team with 4 players in its backfield who would go on to start in the NFL.

But therein was Pete's secret: you don't lose games when you give up just 164 yards against good teams. We'll call it the legacy of Troy Polamalu, who didn't get to play in the last game the previous season—the Orange Bowl—after a reaction to a shot for a hamstring injury. But Troy was there in spirit for this one.

Troy had plenty of disciples on that USC team, though, including defensive linemen Kenechi Udeze, Shaun Cody, and Mike Patterson, who would all go on to All-American careers as big, strong guys who could play fast up front. Behind them were two of the greatest ball hawks in USC history, Matt Grootegoed and Lofa Tatupu. In the back line, as a preview of what was to come by picking off the first pass sent his way as a college athlete that day, was freshman safety Darnell Bing.

On top of all that, USC had a punter that year, also an All-American, in sophomore Tom Malone before a leg injury that would sideline his NFL career. Tommy would average an unheard-of (outside of the Rockies, anyway) 49.0 yards a punt, although he didn't have to do it that often, just over three times a game. It was also Tom's pregame routine of launching bazooka shots way above the top of the Auburn stadium to places these smart SEC fans had never seen a ball kicked. *Who are these guys in Cardinal and Gold?* Auburn fans seemed to be asking themselves as they "oohed" and "ahhed" at one booming punt after another.

Sure, that team also happened to have a couple of budding Heisman Trophy winners in redshirt sophomore Leinart and freshman Reggie Bush, as well as a consensus All-American offensive tackle in Jacob Rogers. But their time to shine would come later.

The team that brought USC back that year was built on defense by a coach, Pete Carroll, who saw the game through a defender's eyes. He promoted a tough-minded, take-no-prisoners attitude. If they can't score, they can't beat you, Pete figured. Like pitching in baseball, defense can always be there. They took the ball away 42 times on turnovers and would produce six All-Americans that 2003 season.

But it was hardly all defense. This USC team would score a Pac-10 record 534 points, and Leinart would become just the second sophomore (John Elway was the other) to be named Pac-10 Offensive Player of the Year after throwing 38 touchdown passes. Leinart and fellow sophomore Williams, who caught 95 passes with a school record 16 for touchdowns, would finish sixth and eighth in the Heisman voting, respectively.

The honors and the deserving Trojans didn't stop there, though. Malone would set the USC punting record. Wide receiver Keary Colbert would set the USC career receiving record. Freshman LenDale White would become the first rookie to lead USC rushing despite sharing the position with Hershel Dennis and another freshman named Reggie Bush. Other major contributors included cornerback Will Poole, center Norm Katnik, and place-kicker Ryan Killeen.

Carroll would be named National Coach of the Year. And for just the second time ever, USC would defeat arch-rivals Notre Dame and UCLA in back-to-back seasons. They then moved on to the Rose Bowl, where a 28–14 win over No. 4 Michigan, after the Trojans had been aced out of the Oklahoma-LSU title game by the BCS computers, would win USC the AP voters' choice as national champions.

Just as Pete Carroll had promised them.

19

USC makes it official with under-the-radar Rose Bowl win

For some reason that no one can quite explain, the 2004 Rose Bowl has become the under-the-radar moment of the last two-plus decades for USC football.

And as hard as it is to believe the victory that would bring home USC's first national championship in a quarter-century could possibly have been somewhat unappreciated, it has been.

Maybe it's because there wasn't just one hero, but many. Or the fact that there was not all that much mystery about the outcome when it came down to it. Sure, USC players and fans were ticked off about the BCS computer shenanigans. But they also knew they had reached that place where Pete Carroll said they would reach, that place where, in the coach's words, they "knew they were going to win."

The pollsters knew, too, obviously. The Trojans had finished No. 1 in the AP media poll and the USC TODAY Coaches Poll. Yet the top-ranked Trojans got shafted when the flawed BCS Rankings kept an Oklahoma team that had lost its last game, 35–7, to Kansas State ahead of them. And advanced the Sooners to the championship game against No. 2 LSU, which had edged USC out by sixteen-hundredths of a point. While it would take some time to sort out, this fiasco would be the beginning of a very long road to the end for the computer-driven BCS rankings that seemed to punish USC inexplicably.

Beating Notre Dame, 45–14, and scoring the most points by a visitor in South Bend in 43 seasons, didn't seem to help USC's ranking. Nor did the Trojans' ability to inflict the worst opening loss ever on Auburn. Nor did romps over Stanford (44–21) or UCLA (47–22). But even worse, the lopsided nature of that Oklahoma loss in the last game of the

Matt Leinart did it all in leading USC to its first national championship in 25 years in 2003 by throwing three TD passes and catching one in a 28–14 Rose Bowl win over Michigan.

season was not factored in as well by rule, just that OU lost. The Sooners would go on to lose to LSU, 21–14, in the BCS championship game.

Only the *New York Times* computer would rank USC No. 1 after the regular season. Two of the six computers would have the Trojans as low as No. 4 and No. 5, while five of the six would agree on Oklahoma as No. 1. It was a strange and difficult year for the numbers-crunchers. *USA TODAY*'s relatively well-respected Sagarin Ratings also missed, ranking the Trojans No. 4 behind No. 3 Miami (Ohio).

Even stranger was the way the BCS computers misfigured USC's strength of schedule. Until late in the day on that final Saturday of the regular season, the computers still had USC with one of the spots in the championship game. But those two late games—Notre Dame at Syracuse and Hawaii-Boise State—saw both USC opponents tank, dropping USC behind Nick Saban's LSU team by dropping the value of USC's wins.

LSU, having played the likes of Louisiana-Monroe, Louisiana Tech, and Western Illinois, had played a tougher schedule, the computers said, than a USC team that, in its nonconference games, had beaten the likes of Auburn, Notre Dame, and BYU.

"I don't know how to fix the system other than to play it off," Carroll told the *New York Times*. All-American wide receiver Mike Williams would go into more detail with the Associated Press. "The one thing I think I can say is we are the No. 1 team in the nation and that is undisputed," Williams said. "If we went out and played either one of those teams, we'd give them their best games and we'd probably win. But right now, that's a whole different thing. So we'll just deal with it and move on."

Sports Illustrated's Phil Taylor was definitely not impressed with the process: "Only a system that places more emphasis on formulas than on football could examine three one-loss teams and eliminate the one that lost only in triple-overtime, hasn't lost since September, and blew out its opponent on the pressure-packed final weekend."

USC would, nevertheless, treat the Rose Bowl as another championship game in a wacky season where not only would there be no undefeated team in college football for first time since the 1996 season, there would also be the first split championship since the BCS was created to avoid such things.

But more than that. Three of the coaches voting in the Coaches Poll, despite an obligation by contract to vote the winner of the BCS game No. 1, refused to do so and kept USC No. 1 as they had voted the Trojans in their final regular season vote. They were Lou Holtz of South Carolina, Mike Bellotti of Oregon, and Ron Turner of Illinois.

Top-ranked USC, 11–1, after being snubbed by the BCS, would face No. 4 Michigan, the Big Ten champs, in Pasadena in a classic Rose Bowl matchup that wasn't hard at all for Carroll to sell to his team and USC fans. All USC had to do was win and the AP national title was theirs.

"Out of the way, pal," Mike Williams says to a Washington Husky.

Michigan's retired Hall of Fame Coach Bo Schembechler, who took ten teams to the Rose Bowl in his twenty-one years in Ann Arbor, seemed content with being the underdog. "I love it," he said. "Michigan, back in the Big Ten, we don't go into any games where we're not favored."

But not this time. The seven-point favorite Trojans jumped out to a 21–0 lead. Ultimately, MVP Matt Leinart threw for three touchdowns and caught a fourth (from left-handed wide receiver Williams), as the slower-moving Big Ten champs couldn't keep pace against a USC defense led by the likes of All-American defensive tackle Shaun Cody, who blocked a field goal.

Cody's heroics were complemented by the 12 tackles and an off-the-shoe interception by All-American linebacker Lofa Tatupu, and the 10 tackles, plus 5 deflections, by cornerback Will Poole. USC's current D-line coach and another All-American on that team,

Kenechi Udeze, had 3 of USC's 9 sacks—the most for the Trojans in 12 seasons—against a Michigan team that had allowed only 15 all season.

The stingy Wolverines had also allowed a mere five touchdown passes in 2003 but on this day would yield another four to the Trojans. Keary Colbert, now a USC assistant coach, led the scoring efforts that day by finishing off his career-record total of 207 with a pair of spectacular touchdown grabs. Running back LenDale White recorded his freshman-record fourteenth touchdown on a pass from Leinart as the Trojans cruised out to that early three-touchdown lead into the third quarter.

Colbert closed out his USC career with 6 catches for a career-best 149 yards. His wide receiver mate Williams had 8 for 88 yards. A freshman named Reggie Bush gave a hint of what was to come with his 41 rushing yards, 42 receiving yards, and 49 return yards for 132 total in the game and a USC freshman record 1,331 yards for the season.

But it was Leinart who would be named Rose Bowl MVP for his 23 completions in 34 attempts for 327 yards with no interceptions and a touchdown catch of his own on that slick 15-yard wide receiver throwback pass from Williams to the wide-open quarterback, who had lateraled the ball on a play heading right only to sneak out to the left pylon for the easy completion from Williams.

Like his Trojans team during and after the game, Pete Carroll would have the final word before it: "You have to work within the system that's in place," Carroll said the day after the regular season. "When we play Michigan in the Rose Bowl, we'll be playing for a championship. If you look at the top of both polls, USC is the name you'll see."

"Let's put that into an equation even a BCS computer might understand," *SI* said. "The Sugar Bowl minus USC equals a big mistake."

For the game, maybe, but for a Rose Bowl that turned the Trojans into national champions, USC will say they got it right even if the computers got it wrong.

20

Not good enough: Aaron Rodgers is almost perfect, but…

There have been larger crowds than the 90,008 fans who showed up at the Coliseum on October 9, 2004, when the No. 1 Trojans faced a No. 7 Cal team led by a quarterback whose name we would hear in future years—Aaron Rodgers.

But there was never a crowd louder than the one heard on that day.

At least not at the end, when the outcome was as uncertain as anyone could imagine, with the decibel level rising to the level of the quality of play as the defending national champion and top-ranked Trojans were also defending their 13-game win streak against the last team to beat them a year ago, in Berkeley. Not that this should have been a surprise to anyone. It had been building since that three-overtime win by the Bears in Memorial Stadium a year before.

And then for the first time ever, ESPN's *College GameDay* chose to come to the Coliseum for its early morning pregame show to get fans on the premises in advance. Busloads even came down from Berkeley. This was big.

Cal's coach Jeff Tedford had it going for the Golden Bears. Of course, Pete Carroll's Trojans were rolling toward what USC fans were seeing as a second straight national championship. They were right.

This was a team that promised excitement galore. Sure, the NCAA had declared All-American Mike Williams ineligible to return for his junior season as the Trojans headed to the airport for a season-opening trip to Washington, D.C.

Later on, in the sixth game, the fifty-millionth fan to attend a USC game, home and away, would be honored at the Arizona State game. Then the Trojans would end Washington's best-in-the-nation's streak of scoring in 271 games with a 38–0 shutout and then become the first No. 1 team in the nation to visit Pullman's Martin Stadium a week later on a cold night in the Palouse for a 42–12 romp.

And in the weirdest combination of fog and cold in a just-past-Halloween Corvallis night, the Trojans would fall behind the orange-and-black-clad Oregon State Beavers, 13–0, only to score the next 28 straight points to get out of Dodge unbeaten.

Back home, USC would beat Arizona for a Pac-10-record fifteenth straight home win and follow with a 38–10 beatdown of Notre Dame for a school-record twenty-first straight home win. Two things were noteworthy about that game: Trailing 10–3, USC scored the final 38 points in a cold, rainy Coliseum. And so much had the ESPN folks enjoyed their early visit, *College GameDay* returned for a second visit.

All that stood between USC and a trip to the BCS championship game that no computer could deny the Trojans this time around was a visit to the Rose Bowl and a season-ending Crosstown Rivalry game against UCLA. The 29–24 win wasn't what USC fans were hoping for. But it was enough. Miami would need to get ready for the 12–0 Trojans.

But it took some serious last-second heroics that October afternoon in the Coliseum against Cal to make it all possible. And as much as USC's season-long motto was "Leave No Doubt," that was hardly the case in the Cal game. There was doubt galore. Not to mention the noise.

Well, it took some doing to get there. Unlike the previous two times these teams had played, USC actually got off to a good start, leading, 10–0, after the first quarter. But that was as comfortable as the Trojans would get in a game where Aaron Rodgers made it clear they'd better not.

All the Cal quarterback did was hit on his first 23 passes, tying an NCAA record, against a "bend-don't-break" USC defense that seemed to be taking that principle to ridiculous lengths in a 16–10 first half in which the Trojans were outgained but somehow still ahead. This was the case thanks to Ryan Killeen's three field goals and a short Leinart-to-LenDale White scoring pass after a Cal punter dropped the snap, giving the Trojans a short field.

But Cal was not going away in this first matchup in 52 years when both teams were ranked in the Top Ten. A pair of familiar names traded scores in the third period with USC getting theirs on a 16-yard Matt Leinart-to-Dwayne Jarrett touchdown pass and the Bears getting theirs on a two-yard Marshawn Lynch TD plunge.

There it would stay, with USC leading, 23–17, until the final 1:47. Rodgers would not go away. If he didn't throw the ball away purposely, which he did twice, he completed every pass he threw—29 out of 29. Perfection. And now, in the hot late afternoon sun, with the shadows coming in at the closed end of the Coliseum, Cal was lining up with a

All-American defensive lineman Shaun Cody helped the Trojans get it together at the end to hold off the near-perfect performance of Cal quarterback Aaron Rodgers.

first down at the USC nine, down 23–17, just a touchdown and extra point away from knocking the Trojans off their perch two straight seasons.

All-American defensive lineman Shaun Cody said it for himself, his teammates, and the 90,008 mostly Trojans fans in the Coliseum: "I was running on empty, our defense was running on empty, but I knew they weren't going to score." USC fans weren't so certain, as the sound waves came cascading down to the field when Cal lined up for a final winning push. USC needed the fans' help. And they were ready.

Was this as loud as anyone had ever heard it in the Coliseum? No one could remember a single more noise-filled four plays. You could barely be heard by the person standing next to you even when you were shouting.

"It's frustrating as a defense when a guy is on fire like that," Cody said of Rodgers. "You've just got to hold on and try to do something to stop them from the end zone." But what?

But this. Rodgers finally missed a pass he intended to complete on first down. For the first time in the game, he threw an incompletion. Second and nine. And then Cal may have reached a bit with all that frenzied sound coming down—and all that pressure to make a play. The Bears tried a shovel pass, but a little-used but extremely talented Trojans defensive tackle out of Long Beach Poly, Manuel Wright, came at Rodgers as if his six-foot-six, 290-pound frame had been shot out of a cannon, getting to the quarterback and sacking him for a loss of five yards. Troy was alive.

A Trojans team that hadn't recorded a single first down in the fourth quarter would make its stand on defense. Cal had already missed a 36-yard field goal with 6:53 left. And now they had a mere 2 downs to go those last 14 yards as the proximity to the end zone seemed to be shrinking the sound-washed Coliseum turf.

One more throw into the end zone came up incomplete again, and Cal called a time-out. There would be one last play. Rodgers would go to his favorite target, Geoff McArthur, who had caught 2 passes for 30 yards to get Cal to the 9. But the ball zipped by, skidding on the turf, and just behind a diving McArthur in the end zone as Rodgers hurried his throw against a USC inside rush. It was over. The Trojans had survived. They would live to play another day.

"Bend but don't break, that's what this game became," USC's Carroll said. Aaron Rodgers had a different take. "We expected to win when we took the field [for that last drive]," Rodgers recalled, as reported by the Associated Press. "I said, 'We're going to go 65 yards right here and get the win.' It's just frustrating that we couldn't get the job done." Fifty-six yards is as far as they got, before USC's sound machine stopped them.

"Anybody watching this game knows we really dominated the game," Rodgers said. "We just came up a little short in the score."

But not on the stat sheet.

USC wasted an opportunity to go up by 2 touchdowns in the second half after an 84-yard Reggie Bush kickoff return when Leinart's tipped pass was intercepted in the end zone. There were few other chances in a game where Rodgers finished with 267 yards passing on those 29 completions with 1 touchdown to Leinart's 164 yards on 16 of 25 passing.

It was worse on the ground. The Bears rushed for 157 yards to just 41 for a stuck-in-place USC that ended up outgained 424 yards to 205.

"The last two weeks have been a battle to the end," Leinart said, after the comeback needed to beat Stanford, 31–28, the week before. But all that mattered was the win. Forget the stats. USC was alive. And on its way.

"I'm so excited I can hardly talk," Leinart said.

Not surprisingly, so were many of the cheered-out USC fans who deserved as much credit this day as any player or coach.

After all, something stopped Cal those final four plays.

A Trojans wall of sound is as good an explanation as any.

21

Sooners had no idea, Trojans had no regrets

If you were one of the thousands of Southern Californians in South Florida the first week of 2005 for the Orange Bowl and had been waiting a full year longer than you should have had to for your Trojans to get a spot in the BCS Championship Game, you knew your time had come.

Because as things played out, you knew something that many of the smart guys, the insider types, the pundits from the rest of the country, and the bettors, who had driven the line down to barely favoring USC, did not get about your top-ranked Trojans. They did not seem to understand, despite the top-ranked Trojans' 21-game winning streak and potential wire-to-wire AP national championships.

Not to mention the fact that the Trojans boasted a backfield featuring Heisman Trophy winner Matt Leinart and the next year's winner (tailback Reggie Bush), as well as the nation's Coach of the Year (Pete Carroll). They also featured an unprecedented six first-team All-Americans (D-linemen Shaun Cody and Mike Patterson and linebackers Matt Grootegoed and Lofa Tatupu in addition to Leinart and Bush). These were not just a bunch of Hollywood pretty boys.

Two things set this USC team apart from the flashy image that preceded the Trojans. They were in the Top Ten in every national statistical defensive category—despite playing in the offensive-minded Pac-10. The Trojans were No. 1 against the run and in turnover margin and No. 3 in total defense while holding opponent offenses to their lowest output in 15 years. As noted, 4 of the Trojans' first-team All-Americans played defense.

Then there was this: this Trojans team arrived in South Florida with an Everglades-sized chip on its shoulder after what the BCS computers did to them a the year before, putting

USC's 2004 national champions.

undeserving Oklahoma and LSU teams into the championship game and forcing the Trojans to win the national championship in the AP Poll—and at the Rose Bowl. This time it would be settled on the field, and that was fine with these Trojans. That's just the way they wanted it.

But with their two-Heisman backfield and an offense that was outscoring opponents by 25.2 points a game—with 8 wins by more than 30 points, it was hard not to focus on the Trojans when they had the ball. They'd scored a combined 70 points in beating archrivals Notre Dame and UCLA for an unprecedented third straight season. Should they keep it going, they would become only the second team ever to go No. 1 preseason to postseason for the AP.

Or was that all smoke and mirrors, as Oklahoma defensive end Larry Birdine indicated earlier in the week when he called Leinart "an overrated quarterback for an average offense"? Birdine wasn't alone. In quieter language, and the closer it got to game day, the more you were hearing the questions. Were the Trojans as "tough" as the 12–0 Sooners, who had been to the title game the year before? Were they as "physical" as an Oklahoma team with NFL draft picks everywhere you looked starting with their own All-American tailback, first Heisman runner-up Adrian Peterson?

Plus if you wanted a Heisman-winning quarterback, the Sooners had one of their own from 2003, and the 2004 second-runner-up, Jason White. And falling short a year ago, the Sooners were equipped with shoulder chips as well in this first-ever game to feature back-to-back Heisman winners against each other and four of the top-five finishers in the Heisman race (Bush was fourth runner-up).

From the media in town, there was an undertone that became a bit louder as they watched USC's loose, open, fun-filled South Florida workouts attended also by large crowds of fans, as well. "That's not the way Oklahoma does it," one Oklahoma City columnist told a home-state sports talk radio audience. "They're much more serious than USC." How exactly he would know that, since the Oklahoma practices were closed and no one got to see them, he couldn't really say. But he was sure they were.

As was the entire Oklahoma fan base, it seemed. This was not even going to be close, they had convinced themselves. And as it turned out, they were right. USC was guilty of having too much fun. Although the USC fun took a bit of a break on Oklahoma's game-opening 92-yard scoring drive for a 7–0 early lead, and the smart guys—and the Sooners fans—nodded knowingly. "See, we told you so."

That was especially so in those early Internet fan board days on the Oklahoma sites where hundreds, thousands even, of Sooners fans had started proclaiming their total, absolute supremacy.

And then it happened . . . or USC happened, actually, as the combination of Leinart's pinpoint-accurate passing, an underrated receiving corps, and the nation's top takeaway specialists in Cardinal and Gold took over.

The Trojans would score the next 28 points and score 38 by halftime, mostly off turnovers with the likes of USC defenders Grootegoed, Eric Wright, and Jason Leach picking off interceptions or picking up fumbles. The final tally had the Trojans with 5 takeaways and no turnovers.

But there was no doubt about the turnover that mattered the most. With the score tied at 7–7 and a USC punt rolling dead near the Oklahoma goal line, Sooners return man Mark Bradley decided unwisely to try to pick it up, surrounded by Trojans. It did not go well, as he lost the handle on the football and any of a half-dozen Trojans could have fallen on it. Backup safety Josh Pinkard did, and on the next play, White scored from the six. The rout was on.

"Just a bonehead play," Bradley said after the game. "I don't know what I was thinking."

What the USC defense was thinking was that this was about more than turnovers, even if the Trojans would score 31 points off them. It was about stopping the run, which had defenders Cody and Patterson arriving at Peterson at the same time White was getting the football to him, meaning that the yardage the star Sooner back was getting was just as likely to be straight up into the air, where the punishing Trojans seemed to be launching him with regularity, limiting him to 82 yards on 25 carries.

Some kind of fun, all right. Despite what Birdine had said, Leinart would throw for a bowl-record 5 touchdown passes and 332 yards without an interception, including a bowl-record 3 to a healthy Steve Smith.

"He won the Heisman Trophy, so we knew he was good coming in," Oklahoma cornerback Marcus Walker said. "But I didn't know he was that accurate." Whatever it was

Wide receiver Steve Smith, with three touchdown catches, was just too fast and too elusive for Oklahoma's defenders in the Trojans' 55–19 2004 national championship game at the Orange Bowl.

that USC was doing in offensive coordinator Norm Chow's play-action passing game, the Sooners had no answer. "When he's on fire, there's nothing the defense can do but sit back and pray," Bush said.

So maybe there was no answer. Didn't the Sooners have to check LenDale White and Bush first? Exactly. Those first steps toward the line of scrimmage proved fatal for the Sooners secondary as Trojans receivers beat them deep time and again. That included tight end Dominique Byrd, who got it started with a spectacular 33-yard one-handed TD grab, and Dwayne Jarrett, who then ran by the Sooners for an early 55-yard scoring strike. Oklahoma hadn't seen guys like that in the Big 12.

"And we thought Oklahoma would have the better receiving corps in this game," ABC play-by-play announcer Brad Nessler said, echoing the prevailing wisdom that had brought so much comfort to the Sooners fans all month and by halftime had exited Pro Player Stadium, much as the Sooners were heading off the field, trailing 38–10 at that point.

Bob Stoops's team would be forced to leave accompanied by the loudest, longest, most sustained boo at any big game in memory that extended fittingly to a disaster of a halftime show. With breakdowns in the sound system—and her voice—singer Ashlee Simpson would suffer a moment almost as ugly as that first half had been for Sooners fans. But even with the lights turned out in the stadium, it might not have been as dark a place as the fans sitting at home posting on the Sooners sites that took a sharp descent into despair seldom plumbed on the Internet.

"I feel sorry for the crowd," Bush would say later. "People paid hundreds or thousands of dollars for tickets and didn't see much of a game."

As for all that fun USC fans and players were having during the week, you could multiply it by whatever number you chose once the game was underway.

Bush racked up 149 all-purpose yards against the stuck-in-the-mud Sooners, while LenDale White added 118 on the ground and place-kicker Ryan Killeen, with field goals of 42 and 44 yards and 7 extra points, became USC's all-time leading scorer. In all, USC would average an incredible 8.3 yards a play piling up 525 yards against an Oklahoma defense that, whatever it was doing during the week, wasn't nearly enough.

Chow was able to do whatever he chose to do on offense, and he chose to throw it first, then run it, on an Oklahoma defense that hadn't given up a touchdown in its last three games. The reverse was not true. Despite running 76 plays, Oklahoma managed just 372 yards (a 4.9 average) with just 118 on the ground, the same as LenDale White gained in 15 carries himself, 10 fewer than Peterson's carries.

"I think we proved tonight that we are the No. 1 team in the country—without a doubt," Leinart said of the Trojans' bowl-record 55 points (the most ever allowed by

Oklahoma in a bowl game). Nevertheless, that 55–19 final score could have been worse had the Trojans not called off the dogs leading, 55–10, with 10:00 left in the game. "We just got whipped," Oklahoma's Stoops said. "You really soul search as a coach how this could happen."

As *Oklahoman* columnist Berry Tramel put it, "It looked like it would be an unforgettable night from the beginning—and that it was." But not the way the Sooners expected. "The night started so gloriously for all things Sooner," he wrote. And then . . .

"They can get on a roll like that where they're good enough as it is," Stoops said of a Trojans team way better than anyone from Oklahoma really seemed to understand, until it was too late. "And then you're contributing to it with your own turnovers and mistakes. It happens quickly, and it doesn't take much."

Actually, it did take a lot. In fact, it took a Trojans team on its way to a second national title posting its twenty-second straight win thanks to a defense no one seemed to realize how talented it was and an offense as good as advertised. And it took a coaching staff just hitting its stride with Pete Carroll's twin mantras of "Competition is Everything" and "Win Forever."

22

The beat goes on, the offense drops seventy on Arkansas

With USC leading the championship game in January 2005 by 38–10 at halftime, most of what the ABC broadcast crew, including USC's now-director of athletics, Lynn Swann, were left to talk about was the next season and a dynasty that could win an unprecedented three straight national titles should quarterback Matt Leinart decide to return the following season—which he did.

For most of the next seven months, that was the talk: dynasty. LenDale White, and all his scoring and rushing records, would return, as well. He and tailback Reggie Bush were just juniors.

In all, eleven players on that 2005 Trojans team would be named first-team All-American sometime in their careers with a USC-record-tying six doing so in 2005. Wide receiver Dwayne Jarrett joined Bush as a unanimous pick in addition to three-time All-American tackle Sam Baker and Leinart, a two-time All-American. Offensive guard Taitusi Lutui and safety Darnell Bing were the final two to earn the honors that year.

All-Americans-in-waiting included center Ryan Kalil, tight end Fred Davis, linebacker Keith Rivers, nose tackle Sedrick Ellis, and wide receiver Steve Smith, the hero of the Orange Bowl national championship game along with Leinart. Only one other team had gone wire-to-wire, first-to-first in AP balloting as USC had in 2004. Could the Trojans be the first to do it two straight seasons?

They would certainly try. For that reason, there was a lot of buzz after a trip to Hawaii for what would be more of a summer-practice-ending scrimmage of an opener in Aloha Stadium, where the 63–17 score didn't say all that much. But in Week Three, there was a legitimate Southeastern Conference opponent that could be seen as a challenge, and for

Offensive tackle Sam Baker was USC's second three-time All-American and a big reason why those Trojans teams in 2005, 2006, and 2007 were so formidable scoring the football.

the first time since that glorious January night in Miami, the Trojans would be back in the LA Memorial Coliseum.

Arkansas Coach Houston Nutt was thrilled at an opportunity no Southeastern Conference team has had since 2005—the chance to walk his team down and through the famed tunnel. Arkansas had been part of USC's national championship history, playing the Trojans in both 1972 and 1974, with a win in 1974, USC's only loss in the 1974 national championship season.

"This is great," Nutt would say on the Friday walk-through as he tried to appreciate the historic Coliseum. He was like a kid visiting Disneyland as he took it all in. His 1–1 Razorbacks were big underdogs, despite the fact that they were leading the nation in rushing and had legitimate big-time threats in tailback Darren McGavin and speedster Felix Jones.

As it turned out, for this Arkansas team, it was a case of wrong place, wrong time, wrong opponent, producing a final 70–17 score so one-sided you'd have to go back to 1918 in the Arkansas record book to find anything worse.

"The best team I have ever seen," Nutt said of the Trojans, who scored 9 of the first 10 times they had the ball and on all 4 possessions in the first quarter when they put up 28 points in just over a minute and a half to score 4 times in 1:32. That's right, it took USC 8 plays to record 4 TDs—all in just 1:32. The crowd of 90,411, described by the Associated Press as "ecstatic," very much approved.

As Nutt described it, "They have all the weapons you need or could hope for. They can score so fast, it messes you up. We had the score 7–7, the next thing we knew, it was 21–7. Leinart is a coach on the field, he is a true playmaker. We wanted to run, but we could not, being that far behind. I'm worried about the psyche of our defense, I hope we can get our confidence back."

Confidence was certainly not a problem for the Trojans, though, who were plenty confident despite the departure of offensive coordinator Norm Chow from the national championship team the year before and replacement by the young Sarkiffians—Lane Kiffin and Steve Sarkisian—whom Carroll wanted to showcase as the new offensive caretakers.

"How much more can you ask of your offense?" Carroll wondered after the Trojans racked up 736 yards on the Razorbacks, more than they'd ever given up anywhere to anybody in their entire history. "This was even more than we could have pictured . . . Arkansas always played such aggressive pass defense, we didn't think it would happen like this."

Maybe "not like this," but they thought it would happen. Here's how it happened. Leinart was 18 of 24 for 381 yards and 4 touchdowns. Bush had 125 yards and a TD on just 8 carries. White had 2 touchdown runs. Steve Smith tallied 4 catches for 129 yards.

Dwayne Jarrett had 2 touchdown catches. And for good measure, Mario Danelo kicked a USC-record 10 extra points.

Yet as exciting as it was to see the return of so much offense, gone were four All-American defenders from the previous season. D-linemen Shaun Cody and Mike Patterson would depart, as would linebackers Lofa Tatupu and Matt Grootegoed. And even though they would hold the Razorbacks to 326 yards, this would be a different USC team that would have to win a different way.

Gone also was top recruiter and D-line coach Ed Orgeron, off to become head coach at Ole Miss. So the defense would need some help should the offense not be able to sustain after that 70-point outburst against Arkansas for the Trojans' twenty-fourth straight win and twenty-second at home.

And score they would, racking up 45 points against Oregon, 38 against Arizona State, 42 against Arizona, 34 against Notre Dame, 51 against Washington, 55 against Washington State, 51 against Stanford, 35 against Cal, 50 against Fresno State, and 66 against UCLA.

But yes, maybe a season-long crack may have been showing. How they won at Notre Dame, 34–31, still mystifies anyone who's ever heard of the "Bush push" or "fourth and nine." And yes, that Reggie Bush offensive outburst against Fresno State may have won him the Heisman, but against a Bulldogs team that put up 42 points, USC had to score 50 to survive.

Now if only they could have put up another 50 in the game that mattered most when their defense couldn't hang in there with Texas and Vince Young in the Rose Bowl, they would have managed a "Three-Peat" that would never be forgotten. But winning with all offense can be tricky. Sometimes the other guys can score, too.

Nevertheless, for the final 12 of USC's 34-game win streak, the Trojans were going to win with offense—until they couldn't.

But that thought was far from anyone's mind on that warm September night in the Coliseum in 2005, when 70 points were all that mattered.

23

The Bush Push . . .
Did that really happen?

It took two miracle plays in the final seconds, two moments that never have happened, certainly not to Notre Dame, and not in a game like this under the gaze of Touchdown Jesus with the Fighting Irish band and fans rushing the field to celebrate a victory they thought was in their grasp . . . but was not to be.

Cheer for Notre Dame all you want, but USC wasn't giving this one back, and no one among the 80,795 who were there will ever forget it how it went down. Not in the stadium that Knute Rockne built. Not against their eight-decade archrival from the West Coast. Not on grass that had been allowed to grow to the length of the US Open rough. Not among the thirty million viewers who would make it the most-viewed college football game in nine seasons.

It was a matchup of two Top Ten teams going head-to-head with ESPN's *College GameDay* on the scene for the second time in the first six weeks of the 2005 season to see if the top-ranked Trojans could pull off their thirteenth straight road win—and twenty-seventh overall—against a No. 9 Notre Dame team that had lost three straight games to Carroll's USC teams by 31 points in each game. This was a big, big deal—something that the Trojans learned only too well as they arrived at the stadium Friday for their walk-through only to have Notre Dame students start rocking the USC buses as they crawled through the crowds outside. So much did the Trojans players like the feel of that, they did it themselves from the inside of their buses on Saturday before the game, clearing their own path to the stadium.

Hall of Famer alums Anthony Munoz and Joe Montana were on hand to greet the players, with Montana the guest star for that night's pep rally moved to the stadium because of the tens of thousands of Irish fans who were coming. For the USC-Notre Dame series, the national attention and impact dated back to the early days in 1927 and 1929, when the teams played in front of 112,000 and 120,000 in Chicago's Soldier Field with New York Yankees immortals Babe Ruth and Lou Gehrig, at the height of their careers, showing up at the pregame luncheon in full USC and Notre Dame game uniforms.

Those Notre Dame uniforms, after the Irish warmed up in their regular home blue jerseys, had turned into the famed green jerseys when they returned to the field. The Irish were pulling out all the stops.

If Lou and The Babe had been around in 2005, they'd probably have been there, as well. Daniel "Rudy" Ruettiger of movie fame was emceeing the pep rally. It had to end up being fun, even if Notre Dame had Coach Charlie Weis's "decided schematic advantage" on offense. As it turned out, for most of a game where USC's defensive shortcomings were starting to become apparent, it looked like the Irish, with Brady Quinn at quarterback, did have an advantage.

What it did not look like was a game that would go against all the lore of the annals of the Golden Dome, a game where it looked like Knute Rockne had given his "Win One for the Gipper" speech to the wrong team, and one where USC's Trojans can boast for all time the single most dramatic, improbable, against-all-odds finish in the history of that legendary place—and maybe in all of college football. But that's what happened.

It was a game so one-of-a-kind, it has its own Wikipedia page. "The Game of the Century," ESPN billed it. And despite a couple of big USC mistakes—a Matt Leinart interception in the Notre Dame end zone that cost USC a touchdown and a Notre Dame punt return TD—USC trailed just 21–14 at the half thanks to Reggie Bush's 36-yard TD scamper that had him hurdling an Irish defender for the score and a LenDale White goal-line blast. Bush would run for 45 yards and a game-tying TD in the third quarter, when the offenses stopped after another Leinart interception and a Keith Rivers forced fumble against the Irish.

Notre Dame jumped out first in the fourth on a field goal before Bush finished off an 80-yard USC scoring drive from 9 yards out to make it 28–24 USC. But then Quinn, playing like the player Notre Dame always hoped he would be, completed 4 passes for 53 yards and then ran it in from the 5 for the go-ahead TD with 2 minutes left. Notre Dame 31, USC 28. Time was running out on the Trojans as the shadows lengthened in the stadium. It was do or die for all those USC streaks.

Hundreds of Irish fans, students, and band members had moved out onto the field hoping to witness up close their team's heroics fully play out in front of them.

Leinart threw an incompletion, was sacked, and on third down hit Bush for 11 yards at the 26, where it was "Fourth and nine" time for the Trojans.

And then it happened. Leinart came to the line of scrimmage, saw single coverage on All-American wide receiver Dwayne Jarrett, and audibled to a fade route to him on which everything would ride.

When Leinart let it go, it looked like the ball was headed right toward the golden helmet of one Ambrose Wooden, the same player Bush had leaped over for USC's first score. This time, Leinart's pass would almost scrape the gold paint off Wooden's helmet as he closed his arms a split-second too late to prevent the ball from getting to Jarrett's hands before he took off in a 61-yard foot race down the sideline with the entire Notre Dame secondary—not to mention sideline media—in pursuit. They would catch him at the 13.

"You just have to throw it up there and hope he gets it," Leinart said. "I'll take my chances with him against anyone in the country. He made a play."

But it wasn't over yet. Nor was it over after two Bush carries had gotten the ball to the two-yard line. A Leinart scramble to the sideline had the ball popped loose out of bounds past the downs marker somewhere near the one-yard line with :07 left. Only no one seemed to have told the Notre Dame clock operator, who allowed the time to run out on the board and thousands of Irish students and band members rushed the field while one USC beat reporter made his way up the now-open sidelines to get to the goal line for what was going to happen next. He was sure there would be at least one more play.

Good thing he didn't wait, because all those people out on the field were told that sorry folks, this game isn't over. It was USC's ball with those seven seconds left after Carroll had sprinted down the sideline to confer with the temporarily confused officials. Carroll appeared to be signaling Leinart to spike the ball and kill the clock for the timeout USC did not have. Only Notre Dame should have realized that Carroll would go for the win, fake killing the clock, and roll the dice. In the huddle, Bush told Leinart to go for it, which the quarterback did, sneaking it to the left, where he was stonewalled. Stay there and the game was over. No field goal. No tie. Just a staggering loss.

But Leinart didn't stop. He spun and came back right where Reggie Bush was ready to push him home. Which he did. It was finally over. USC 34, Notre Dame 31. Forget the extra point, the celebration penalty, and the kickoff. The game was over at that moment.

"I used all 200 pounds of my body to push Matt in," Reggie said. And that was it.

"I just saw it, I thought it was there and I just wanted to get in," Leinart said. "I didn't want to spike the ball, so I made the choice and they were looking down from above and we got in. That was all that mattered."

Indeed. USC's 5,000 fans seemed joyously immobilized in their corner section seats right where Leinart had scored. They were not leaving. Hold that alumni train to Chicago. It was time for a little celebrating in South Bend—or a whole lot—as the Trojans Marching Band would not stop playing. And the USC players, replacing those suddenly sad Irish

Pete Carroll and center Ryan Kalil showing the euphoria that swept Troy after the "Bush Push" and the improbable 34–31 win over Notre Dame in South Bend in 2005.
Associated Press

students, had taken over the field and they were not leaving. All realized the historic nature of what had happened here. This was a Notre Dame program that had ended historic streaks for Oklahoma, Army, Texas, and 32 years earlier, for USC. So exactly how it had happened was a bit murky. Had these Trojans really seen what they just saw? Stuff like that does not happen to Notre Dame on Knute Rockne's turf.

"You gotta believe you're going to win the way that happened," Carroll said. Yes you do. USC did. But it was a different story for Notre Dame. "People were pretty shocked and devastated," Irish quarterback Quinn said, seeing how the "exact opposite" of what had brought the fans out on to the field had happened a bare two minutes later.

But what about the "Bush push," Notre Dame fans wanted to know. Is that legal? Doesn't the rule book say that "the runner shall not grasp a teammate; and no other player of his team shall grasp, *push* [emphasis added], lift or charge into him to assist him in forward progress"? But it's almost never called. As Weis said in generous remarks in his postgame press conference, in that same situation, he'd hope his running back would do the same as Bush did—a classy move defusing any sour grapes at USC's victory.

As Weis spoke, the celebrations went on into the darkness with the stadium lights providing a halo effect for the folks in Cardinal and Gold. They would remember this feeling for a long, long time—and then some.

This is what "Fight On" feels like, what it looks like, what it sounds like—and what happens when it comes to life in a moment like this.

"I had no doubt," Bush said. "We never gave up and kept fighting. That's why we're the No. 1 team in the country."

But as much as the entire Trojans party had come together, Carroll and his fan base finished up in a different place. "We'll be happy to leave South Bend," Carroll said. His USC fans would not be. They wanted to stay and sing "Fight On" and hear "Conquest" and "Tusk" one more time until they turned the lights out.

24

Reggie wins his Heisman . . . and does so against Fresno State

Who would have thought it would have come down to this? That Reggie Bush, with his brilliant three-year college career and all those one-of-a-kind games for all the national championship marbles, against all those Power Five programs, would clinch his 2005 Heisman Trophy against . . . the Fresno State Bulldogs.

But that's exactly what happened that November 19 night in front of 90,007 at the Coliseum. Not to put down the No. 16 Bulldogs of Pat Hill. Those guys could play. Only three other USC opponents—No. 9 Notre Dame, No. 14 Arizona State, and No. 11 UCLA—were ranked higher on the regular season schedule. And as the year went on, it was becoming more and more obvious that this USC team, with its injuries and inexperience, couldn't play much defense.

But boy, could those Trojans score points—63 against Hawaii, 70 against the SEC's Arkansas, 51 against Washington and Stanford, 55 against Washington State, and 66 against archrival UCLA. So maybe it shouldn't have been shocking that they would score 50 points against the No. 16 Bulldogs in the second-to-last game of the regular season.

What was shocking was that they had to score that many in this game. That wasn't the case in any of those other scoreboard busters that saw USC win those six games by an average of forty-and-a-half points.

That would not be the case in a come-from-behind 50–42 USC win that seemed much closer than that final score suggests. It was during that win that Reggie Bush's "One Shining Moment," to quote the title of that CBS "March Madness" theme, would take place. The fifth in the line of USC's Heisman Trophy-winning tailbacks and second straight San Diegan—following Mike Garrett (1965), O.J. Simpson (1968), Charles White (1979),

Flying with both feet off the ground, Reggie Bush had a once-in-a-career game against Fresno State in 2005.

and Marcus Allen (1981)—Bush would demonstrate all the skills that USC recruits, to this day, cite as the moment they first found the Trojans program, even though many were early grade-schoolers at the time.

Reggie Bush may have had all the flash anyone could imagine as possibly college football's most electric, multiskilled offensive player ever. Bush managed to serve as running back, receiver, punt returner, kickoff returner— pretty much whatever was needed of him—but he also has plenty of staying power. This remained the case, despite the forced return of his Heisman Trophy after the NCAA's finding in 2010 that his family received illegal benefits from would-be agents who hoped to sign Reggie as a client once he left college.

None of that mattered on November 16, 2005, on a relatively muggy night at a nearly jam-packed Coliseum where thousands of Fresno folks had made their way more than 200 miles downstate to see what they hoped would be the upset of all upsets. The way USC's defense had devolved, the Fresno folks weren't all that far off the mark—at least with the hope. It wasn't a bad bet. They had a shot.

Except for one force that might have gotten in their way: Reggie Bush, the six-foot, 200-pound junior speedster who may have been at the height of his powers that night. Because he had to be. All those practices over all the years when Pete Carroll would call a full-speed Reggie blast into the first-team defense's line of scrimmage and Reggie would hit it up in there on the day's first play—day after day after day, season after season after season. No better way to start the day with a Reggie blast of practice energy.

Which is what often got lost in any analysis of Reggie Bush. Sure, he had the speed and skill set, the stop-and-start, change-of-direction talent, the hands to catch it, the feet and balance to cut with it, the legs to power through it to go the distance, and the determination not to let up.

But even more, Reggie had—and this has been well-documented—an unparalleled work ethic from the time his mother allowed him at the age of eight to take up the game he loved. "You saw Reggie Bush practice?" the star running back of the 2017 Trojans, Ronald Jones, asked in wonder and awe when he was told that something he did reminded a longtime USC observer of how Reggie did it. He didn't care about putting him into a Reggie Bush story, just about hearing about Reggie Bush from someone who saw him up close. It made him remember, Ronald said, the first time the Texan saw Reggie in that year's Rose Bowl when he was just eight.

With the game getting much less exposure on FSN, Bush toiled a bit in anonymity in this game. But his Pac-10 record 513 yards on 294 yards rushing on 23 carries, his 68 receiving yards on three catches, and his 135 yards in kickoff returns and another 16 returning punts said it all for him in what Fresno State Coach Pat Hill called "a fifteen-round slugfest." That was 145 yards more than any Trojan had ever put up in a game—the 368 by Anthony Davis in that memorable 55–24 comeback against Notre Dame in 1974.

"I was really feeling it," Bush said, "I was in sync tonight." He was more than that, as Pete Carroll made clear. "He was electric all night long," Pete said of Reggie. "He's just got the magic. You've got to be in love with him. He was firing and roaring."

But mostly, for USC's sake and for that of Reggie himself after his late fumble allowed Fresno the go-ahead score for a 42–41 lead, he didn't let it bother him. "It was just a great football player trying to make something happen," Carroll said. "It broke his heart when he fumbled the ball. But that wasn't the end of the game." Nope.

As soon as the Trojans got the ball back, Reggie escaped out of the backfield and caught a 43-yard wheel route pass down to the FSU 21 yard line, from where USC drove it in for a LenDale White go-ahead score they would not relinquish.

"All the coaches told me to keep my head in the game," Reggie said, "and that's what I did." Fresno's Hill agreed. "Obviously, No. 5 [Bush] is a great, great player. USC showed why they've won 33 games in a row." On offense, anyway. Quarterback Matt Leinart was the reigning 2004 Heisman winner. And with this game, did this push Bush himself to the head of the line for 2005? "I'm not sure if it does. But either way I'm thankful and grateful to my team. My real worry is this team."

"This team really does believe," Carroll said. "They believe in themselves and each other. This was a hard night—a really good job by Fresno. They really made it hard . . . they should be in the Top Ten, easily."

Where his USC team should be, Carroll wasn't so sure, not after the defensive issues they displayed. But for Bush, there was no doubt: "As the season winds down, you hope guys separate themselves and he was awesome today," Pete said. "He was pure magic. He was disappointed with his one play [the fumble], but he's a great player and was just trying a little too hard."

Indeed, the first time he touched the ball, Reggie cruised 65 yards to set up a 5-yard tying TD while getting up to top speed effortlessly as he liked to do and just flying by defenders who couldn't get to Reggie speed. Then he took it 45 yards for a go-ahead score at 27–21, too quick, too sharp an ability to cut back. Then a 50-yard race to the end zone to put USC ahead, 41–28. Then a 65-yard catch when Fresno tried to defend him with a linebacker who had no chance to get the Trojans back in position for the game-winning score late.

Those 513 all-purpose yards absolutely demolished the USC record, although the vindictive NCAA, in banishing Reggie's records to the nonhistory section of the library, would tell you it didn't happen. That Marqise Lee's 468 yards against Arizona in 2012, which included 345 receiving yards and 123 in kickoff returns, should now be listed first in the *USC Media Guide*, the NCAA censors tell us. But as every USC fan, even the ones who were not in the Coliseum that night, knows, 513 yards are more than 468.

Reggie Bush's November 16, 2005, performance was one for the books—even the record books. And always will be.

25

Afraid of the big, bad Horseshoe?
Not these Trojans

How much fun was this going to be for USC fans—a second big trip to the Midwest in the fall, to one more of college football's sacred sites, to that big Horseshoe in Columbus, where a record, and beyond loud, Buckeyes crowd of 106,033 would greet them. And where there would be revenge in Ohio State's mind in 2009 after what a veteran, all-time great USC defensive team had done to the Scarlet and Gray in a 35–3 USC romp the year before in the LA Memorial Coliseum.

Who else but USC would do this—scheduling a game at Ohio State the second week of September and then coming back to the Midwest the third week of October to face Notre Dame? Easy answer: no one else would. No one would even think about trying that kind of double dip. But here the 2009 Trojans were, with a young, untested, hopeful on offense and not all that talented on defense team, somehow still ranked No. 3 in the nation with a freshman quarterback, Matt Barkley, after just one college start. Had USC's 56–3 opening romp over San Jose State really signified anything? Not really.

But this one would. The third-ranked Trojans were up against a revenge-minded bunch of Buckeyes who not only had the prior year to think about, but also the previous six USC-Ohio State matchups, all of which had gone to the Trojans, including three Rose Bowls. Deducting the 5,000 USC fans in attendance, more than 100,000 angry Buckeyes were thinking about nothing else. This was not going to be easy. Should USC have been favored? Maybe only because of Pete Carroll—and the history here. No other reason.

The funny thing about it: this would be Carroll's last big memorable moment as a Trojan for a USC team that would start strong and then take a nose dive on defense so precipitous that it would be part of the rationale for Pete's return to the NFL. His time as a college coach would soon be up. Hello Seattle. Pete was not about coaching a team that allowed 47 points at Oregon and then give up 55 more in the worst Homecoming loss in USC history to Stanford. But that would be in some future moment.

Because as bad as the final-second 16–13 loss the following week at Washington would be for an unprepared USC team with no idea who would start at quarterback for an injured Barkley, the Trojans had rallied their way back to No. 4 in the nation thanks to a 34–27 win over a ranked Notre Dame team in South Bend with Barkley back. USC would join Michigan and Michigan State as the only teams to beat Notre Dame eight straight seasons. Then came Oregon and it all went away. By the time the Trojans were upset in the finale by Arizona at the Coliseum, all that lay ahead of them was the Emerald Nut Bowl in a baseball park in San Francisco in the rain. Going out 9–4 and in a tie for fifth in the Pac-12 was not Pete Carroll's idea of coaching at USC. And within weeks, this was not his team, either.

In contrast, Ohio State would rally under Jim Tressel, get its act together, and by season's end, it would be the Buckeyes—not USC—back in Pasadena. In one of those "You just never know" moments, they would beat an Oregon team that had laid waste to USC, in the Rose Bowl.

But on this September 12 night, that would all be sometime in the unknowable future. This was now, on an almost muggy Ohio evening. It was a time of great, if fleeting, promise for these Trojans—and Carroll—and a wonderful trip to Buckeye-land for USC fans.

For four Trojans who might have been, this would be the game for their memory book. For linebacker Matt Galippo, a third-year player of unlimited potential cut short by a succession of back surgeries, it was a glimpse of what could have been for him when he picked off a Terrelle Pryor pass in the opening minutes and returned it 51 yards to the 2. Taking over there would be senior tailback Stafon Johnson, with a career shortened by a weight-lifting accident, who would drive the ball in for a 7–0 crowd-quieting USC lead. "Not again," you could hear the Buckeyes fan mumbling.

Keeping the Trojans in it long enough for Johnson's second score was the combination of a defense that played far better than it would the rest of the season and Barkley, the Newport Beach kid by way of Mater Dei High School who had just turned nineteen. He would get pounded around and picked off once, but he completed 15 of 31 passes for 195 yards, and, for much of this defensive battle, that's all USC had. He would accomplish this with a numb right shoulder after a big hit earlier in the game.

Meanwhile, the Trojans defenders, led by Galippo, Josh Pinkard, and Taylor Mays, were hanging in there, limiting Ohio State to a tying TD and a go-ahead field goal in the first half that USC would match for a 10–10 intermission tie. The defensive battle, field-position game continued through the third quarter with Ohio State getting a short field goal and a safety after the snap was fumbled into the end zone by USC's Billy O'Malley. And that's the way it would stay. Until . . .

Until what many USC fans would dub "The Drive." USC had "The Comeback" in 1974 in that 55–24 turnaround Notre Dame game (see Chapter 13). They would soon have "The Drive," as well as a memory of Joe McKnight, in his junior season, showing flashes of the ability that had him the nation's top-ranked running back coming out of John Curtis High School in New Orleans three years earlier. And with McKnight's untimely death after getting gunned down in a road rage incident last year in New Orleans, it's tragically all they would have.

Everything they would need on a final do-or-die drive in the last minutes as USC would go officially 86 yards on 14 plays for the win. But it was more than that, much more as USC opened what would be a game-winning possession with a 5-yard penalty and a 4-yard sack of Barkley to put the ball back to the 5, where it was second and nineteen with just 6:09 left. The Trojans were 95 yards away as they huddled right in front of the loudest part of that screaming Buckeyes end zone crowd.

"He was scared, really," McKnight kidded with sportswriters about his young teammate, Barkley, after the game. "No, he came with the same composure he had the whole game. He was calm. He made plays." Then McKnight admitted that on this night, unlike his first two years, after he missed the block that allowed the Barkley sack, USC kept him in the game.

In *the* game of his college career, Joe McKnight preparing to take off in leading the Trojans to an 18–15 win in Columbus on a final possession known forever as "The Drive."

Pretty darn smart of the Trojans. Joe liked it too, as his 60 yards rushing on 16 carries would mostly come on this drive when he mixed in speed, power, and elusiveness—and an ability to catch the ball. This was Joe's USC moment. "I'm making up for the two years that I was here, that's what I was doing."

The play-by-play tells it all. McKnight for 11 quick yards to make it third and eight. Then Barkley hit Joe for 21 more against Ohio State defenders simply not quick enough to stay with the elusive back out of the backfield. And someway, somehow, the Trojans had an improbable first down at the 37.

Next up would be a Barkley to tight end Anthony McCoy pass for 26 yards to the Ohio State 37 and there was more than a glimmer of hope for the Trojans, trailing just 15–10. It would take USC all 4 downs to navigate the next 10 yards—a Barkley incomplete pass, a McKnight rush for one, a Barkley-to-Damian Williams pass for 8 yards, and a Barkley sneak for 1 and the first down. Then Joe said to give it to him.

He ran it for four, then nine, then eight. Again, he was just too quick. The ball was on the Ohio State six with 1:14 left—and the Buckeyes were now calling timeout. They knew they were in trouble. From the sounds of the crowd, it was becoming obvious this game was going the wrong way.

Again USC was about to ruin their fun. A Barkley sneak for four gave USC a first down at the two. After Ohio State's next timeout, Stafon Johnson, the end zone finder, came on for a misdirection sweep that had him untouched and arms extended in a crowd-silencing stroll into the end zone. But that wasn't the end of it. Barkley would hit McKnight for the two-point extra point for a three-point margin, making USC field-goal proof with an 18–15 lead that would become the final score after an Ohio State game-ending four and out.

It got downright quiet in The Horseshoe from there. "It was good to hear the silence," Barkley said. And you could hear it. Nothing beats that for a USC team that was winning its tenth straight game against a Big Ten team. "We're Trojans. That's what we do," Barkley said. "This is what we dreamed of, coming back like this. Doesn't matter where we are in the score. We found a way. I love this."

Carroll loved the sound of his young leader, calling it "an incredible accomplishment for any quarterback, anywhere, anytime."

"He's not nineteen, he's our quarterback. I'm not worried about how old he is. Numbers mean nothing." But this is what did, Carroll said of that moment in the third quarter when USC was forced to call a timeout to check out Barkley's right shoulder when he'd lost feeling after getting hit. The *New York Times* reported how Carroll did two things: he got backup Aaron Corp warming up and asked Barkley to squeeze his hand. "There was no way I was going out," Barkley said. "I wouldn't let them."

The final word from Carroll: this wasn't about either Barkley or McKnight alone. "I think it's a beautiful statement for our whole team. It was really a great job by a lot of guys."

That was not the Ohio State sentiment, and for the thousands of USC fans in Columbus, it may be what they most remember—the silence. Then came the attempts to explain by the Buckeyes. "It's very frustrating, but we knew eventually they'd make plays," Ohio State linebacker Brian Rolle told the Associated Press. "The last drive was heartbreaking. Give McKnight lots of credit on that last drive, he was good. The last drive was definitely, you go back and you think about, and you think about how close you came to winning."

But there was another reason. Ohio State's Tressel wasn't afraid to say it. "You need to score more than five points in the second half, and they came up with plays on that last drive they needed to and so they go home with the spoils."

Pryor's take wasn't so generous, but it was a beautiful sound for Trojans fans who had had to listen to a lot of Buckeye noise for more than 58 minutes. "We should have beat them," Pryor said. "Point blank, we should have beat them."

Yet they didn't. USC had one sudden-silencing drive too many for the Buckeyes. "I'm stoked with the victory," Barkley was quoted in the *New York Times*. "I'm going to enjoy it while I can. It's sweet. I'm enjoying every second of it."

26

Did that man in the cardinal-and-white ski outfit just walk away from Eugene a winner?

If this wasn't going to be a victory party for the home-standing Ducks on national TV, then why did Oregon uberbooster alum Phil Knight invite all of his—and Nike's—best friends, starting with LeBron James, down to the Autzen Stadium sidelines?

The No. 18 Trojans, knocked out of the Pac-12 championship game, seemed to have one choice in the cold and the late-night national TV atmosphere at overflowing Autzen Stadium on November 19, 2011: ruin the party for Phil & Friends, as they watched and welcomed it all up close on the field.

The play of this Trojans team had been deceiving up to this point. After all, they'd lost games they shouldn't have, hence the No. 18 ranking. But behind the ferocious blocking of All-American left tackle Matt Kalil and the tough-as-nails multiposition Rhett Ellison, they were as dangerous a team as any in the nation that many argue should have been unbeaten.

Although maybe that needs to be qualified. How do you avoid blips like the horribly sloppy loss in the desert at Arizona State and the curiously officiated triple overtime defeat by No. 4 Stanford in a 56–48 Coliseum thriller?

It's clear the Ducks fans were looking to defeat a USC team against whom they had rung up a cool 100 points the previous two seasons. And despite the cold, those 59,933 Autzen Stadium fans, earmuffs and all in the nation's loudest college football venue, had bundled up to celebrate a Cardinal-and-Gold bonfire. After all, the Ducks had won 21 straight home games, 19 straight Pac-12 games, and 9 straight overall. Just add one more to the fire.

Was Lane Kiffin purposely making a show of how cold it could get in wintry Eugene, Oregon, with his ski-wear attire? He was. And it worked.

As for those highly paid Oregon cheerleaders, LeBron and his buddies had allegedly been working out at Nike headquarters in Beaverton and decided to join their Uncle Phil at his home away from home in Eugene. During a pregame flag football scrimmage, LeBron played quarterback—of course—with his buds Chris Paul, Dwyane Wade, Chris Bosh, Carmelo Anthony, and others, tossing the ball around for fun, with no one on defense.

And then, as so often happens in football fantasies, the game started. Real life intervened. As Brent Musburger and Kirk Herbstreit called it for ABC's *Prime Time*, USC's ski-outfit-wearing head coach, Lane Kiffin, mocked the Oregon winter freeze to send a message to recruits that this gosh-awful cold, windy, and wet part of the world is the last place you'd ever want to end up.

It wasn't all that close—until Lane, suddenly showing fear, and his dad Monte's "bend, bend, bend until you almost break" defense, kicked in. Then luckily for the Trojans at the end, the clock ran out, the final field goal attempt was missed, and the 38–35 USC win was in the books.

Another "U" would be in the *USC Media Guide*. That's the "upset" marker that USC puts next to a score in its season-by-season results section. And since historically, USC hasn't been the underdog all that often, there aren't many of them. For that reason, this night was particularly special.

Perhaps even sweeter for the Trojans was the fact that Oregon, one of USC's Pac-12 buddies who failed to rally around the Trojans when the NCAA came a-callin', was poised to move up to the No. 2 spot in the BCS rankings, with Oklahoma State's earlier loss that day. That would mean the Ducks would have a chance to get back to the championship game. All they needed to do was beat USC, but with the Trojans' win, USC was finally getting around to evening up the account ledger.

For Trojans quarterback Matt Barkley, just a junior but also the chief spokesman for the program, was the man of the hour with his 4 touchdown passes for 323 yards.

"We expected to shock everybody except ourselves," Barkley said after the game as the Trojans thawed themselves out. "I think this was a defining game for us. We set ourselves apart on both sides of the ball." For a while, anyway.

The game represented a joyous jump-out for USC fans that had the Trojans doing pretty much whatever they wanted against the Ducks, leading 24–7 well into the third quarter as Barkley picked apart a less-athletic-than-the-USC-receivers Oregon secondary.

"We needed this," Barkley said. Actually, Barkley needed the wide receiver duo of Serra High alums Robert Woods and Marqise Lee. The sophomore Woods had overcome a week of injuries to his ankle and shoulder without practicing to come on and make one tough catch after another—7 in all, with 2 for touchdowns—while freshman Lee would go 8 for 187 yards and a 59-yard touchdown that got things started.

Woods scored USC's next 2 touchdowns, as the Trojans led 14–0 in the first quarter, then 21–7 at halftime. The first was from the 12-yard line, the second from the 4. An Andre Heidari field goal in the third would make it 24–7, and then a Marc Tyler touchdown run and a 5-yard scoring strike to tight end Randall Telfer as the Trojans piled up 462 yards of offense would push the USC lead out to 38–14 late into the third quarter. But give Kiffin credit for calling this correctly. "I never felt comfortable," he said. "You can't get comfortable. They're just so explosive."

Although until USC called the dogs off, that USC defense did it about as well as you could against the Ducks. Hayes Pullard led the way with 14 tackles, T.J. McDonald added 8 and Dion Bailey 7, and Nick Perry was a force from his end spot.

The Ducks' De'Anthony Thomas was a force as well, with a 96-yard kickoff return for a TD to get the Ducks started, and tailbacks Kenjon Barner and LaMichael Thomas also contributing to the scoring against a USC defense assuming the fetal position to make it 38–35. But none of that would have mattered had USC followed through on its final drive when the offense said to heck with acting scared of the Ducks and drove down to the Oregon 15 with less than 3 minutes left. But thanks to a miscommunication between Barkley and Tyler, the ball on a handoff miscue hit the ground instead of Tyler hitting the hole, and suddenly an Oregon defense unable to stop the Trojans had managed to do just that.

At that point, it was time for Coach Kiffin to hold onto his ski cap, as USC quickly yielded yards to the Ducks before finally forcing them into an attempted game-tying field goal. A USC penalty shortened it from 42 yards to 37 before Alejandro Maldonado hooked it left and the celebrating began. So excited was the USC locker room that university President Max Nikias emerged with a suggestion that Director of Athletics Pat Haden should get the game ball.

Give Oregon's Kelly credit. He came over to the USC locker room to congratulate the Trojans coaches after the game, saying it wasn't a letdown after beating Stanford the week before. "I didn't feel like it was a hangover," he said. "The credit goes to that other team. That's a good football team."

On a night when no one in Oregon thought it was possible—unless they were wearing Cardinal and Gold—that good team managed to come out victorious.

"We lost a football game," Oregon's LaMichael James was quoted later. "Life goes on."

For fans of Trojans football already grappling with the lack of a postseason after the first NCAA penalties for alleged receipt of benefits had kicked in, life would go on. But after that November night in Eugene, Oregon, they'd be going on with a smile on their faces.

27

Coach O's baker's dozen defenders do Stanford in, rock the Coliseum

It was a story of the few . . . and the many. Just six weeks after USC had fired coach Lane Kiffin overnight at LAX after the 2011 Arizona State game, Trojans fans had something to celebrate. And did they ever celebrate!

As they should have. This was happening in the depths of the NCAA-sanctions-diminished rosters when week after week, the number of originally recruited game-eligible USC scholarship players would be down in the midforties, an unheard-of number against teams with 80 to 85 eligible scholarship recruits.

Despite it all, the unranked Trojans were still 7–3, even with a 14–10 loss to Notre Dame in South Bend when they ran out of receivers. But now they'd face a major test. No. 4 Stanford was in town, riding high with four straight wins (and five in the last six) against the Trojans—not an ideal matchup, it would seem, for a limited USC roster that would have to stand up to the pounding physicality of the Cardinal.

As Pac-12 commissioner Larry Scott bragged before the game, the conference could say it was home to "the two top-ranked one-loss teams in America," in reference to Stanford and Oregon. The Trojans seemed to be an afterthought that November night in front of a Saturday evening sellout crowd of 93,607 at the Coliseum.

Although one thing Scott could brag about after the game: the Pac-12 had, without doubt, the best three-loss team in the nation in USC's Trojans. Because after the game, USC's loss total remained at three, although Stanford was no longer a one-loss team. By the next Monday, No. 23 USC would no longer be unranked.

Interim Coach Ed Orgeron was making magic happen here even though he said people were throwing their praise in the wrong direction. "It's not about me," Coach O said

The postgame celebration at the Coliseum after USC upset No. 4 Stanford with an undermanned Trojans team limited by sanctions lifted Coach Ed Orgeron to his greatest win.

after USC's 20–17 last-second win (with 19 seconds on the clock), "it's about them." It was the only call he got wrong all night. After all, it most definitely was about him.

"We absolutely love him," quarterback Cody Kessler said after his 25-of-37 passing performance for 288 yards and a touchdown. "We'd run through a brick wall for him. He has that look in his eyes when he talks to you that he really does care. I gave him a hug after the game and I don't know if he'd want me to say this but I saw his eyes water up. It's awesome when you play with someone who has that same passion."

There was passion everywhere when thousands upon thousands of Trojans fans stormed the field in an unprecedented emotional response to the win and maybe the NCAA's decision on the sanctions. Programs accustomed to winning over the years the way USC had been doing just don't do that sort of thing. But this was different. This wasn't supposed to happen. Stanford had USC's number.

And the one number here that was clear is that this USC defense under coordinator Clancy Pendergast was basically one-deep. Just two subs made it onto the field on defense with Torin Harris playing just a single play. The Trojans' front 7 was intact throughout, as USC played a starting 12 with Dion Bailey revolving in with S'ua Cravens, Demetrius Wright, Kevon Seymour, and Josh Shaw on the back line. That was it—12 plus 1.

For the fifth game the 2013 season, the Trojans would use 3 or fewer defensive substitutions. That, in and of itself, might be the single-most amazing stat imaginable. This was "Fight On" coming to life in one season, on one night. And on that night, USC would hold Stanford to a season-low 17 points and stop a team that had been converting 52 percent of its third-down opportunities to just 4 of 12.

But that wasn't enough. The game was still tied at 17 and it was Stanford's ball late. "We knew we had to do something," Bailey said of his decision to decoy Stanford quarterback Kevin Hogan and then jump the route he'd recognized from an earlier play.

"I told Su'a he wasn't going to have any help," Bailey said of deserting his fellow defender on the edge who had already recorded a Stanford-stopping interception. "I was going for it." And the old Matt Grootegoed/Lofa Tatupu deception trick of looking the opposite way from where he knew the ball would be going worked. After Bailey's pick, it was USC ball.

But it wasn't Bailey's heroic play alone, he said. "Give the guys up front the credit, that ball was coming out quick because they were in on the quarterback."

Now it was USC's turn to make something happen in a game where two pounding defenses were prevailing and USC would gain a minuscule 23 yards on the ground. And then it was fourth and two on the Stanford 48 with just 1:23 left. So what do you do? Do you go for the touchdown, as your players want you to, maybe miss, and watch Stanford go down and kick a field goal, which probably would have happened, just as it had happened in recent losses?

The Trojans would go for it. "I knew I was taking a chance," Orgeron said when he decided to put it on the line for the win. And maybe for his own future as coach. "But I looked in these guys and knew they wanted to go for it. I wanted to give them the best shot to get what they wanted. It worked. It was a great call. It could have gone the other way. I understand that. It was a good throw."

It wasn't just the Cody Kessler throw. There was another dialogue going on in the huddle. Wide receiver Marqise Lee, who had been kicked in the shin a couple of plays earlier and was limping in pain, was telling Cody, "I've got one more play in me." And so he did. Two playmakers came together to make one big play for the first-down conversion and then Kessler would make one more big play, on a scramble pass to Nelson Agholor, who would take it 11 yards for another first down with 43 seconds left at the Stanford 21.

Which is where things got a bit more complicated, as USC proceeded to lose 9 yards on the next two plays before gaining a yard and now on fourth down, would call on Andre Heidari, who had missed his first extra point of the night, for a 47-yard game-winning field goal. It was similar to the one he almost got to try two years ago against Stanford, when the officials decided the clock had run out in regulation.

On this particular occasion, there was plenty of time to spare. And he had plenty of leg, Heidari said, as soon as he hit what would be USC's first game-winning last-second field goal in 13 seasons, looked up, and saw it heading right down the middle of the crossbar: "I started running back . . . I knew I had plenty of leg."

Just as on this night, and under this coach, USC had plenty of heart to match those playmakers who stepped up on both sides of the ball. Cravens had another line of postgame rhetoric that didn't work out. "Coach O needs to be here next year, that's all I've got to say," the freshman defender said, and then he said it again, "He's a players' coach."

Not to mention he was 5–1 in his six-game season after taking over a train wreck from Lane Kiffin. "He's loosened us up," Heidari said.

For Soma Vainuku, who scored his first career touchdown in the first quarter on a 1-yard pass reception when USC put up 14 points on a Stanford team that had given up just 24 all season in the first quarter of its 9 previous games, the change in playmaking was palpable. "It's amazing," Soma said of the chance to make up for his dropped end zone pass a year ago against Notre Dame. "I can't explain it. Last year was last year. We're utilizing all our guys now." One of those was tailback Javorius "Buck" Allen, who got his first career start and scored a TD in the first quarter, as well.

But maybe most amazing of all might have been those thousands of USC fans rushing the field and not wanting to leave. It's the last place they thought they'd be, and the joy that was being shared, from player to fan to family—the Trojans family—was something most of them had never been a part of. Not like this. "We wanted to beat them so bad," Bailey said of a Stanford team with a 12-game in-state win streak. "No way we should have been losing to them. This one is for our class that had never beaten them. We knew we had to make plays and we did."

"One team, one heartbeat," Hayes Pullard repeated what Coach O had been preaching to them. It was more than a slogan, he said. "We wanted that to carry over. When you have a father figure like Coach O treating us all like his sons and putting us under his arm . . . we wanted to show him that we are with him no matter what."

Stanford Coach David Shaw, in a classy postgame move, spent eight futile minutes trying to locate Orgeron after the game but could not find him on the fan-filled field. So he eventually made his way to the USC locker room to offer his congratulations. "Everybody, except for the people in this conference, is surprised by USC," Shaw said.

That wasn't the case for Shaw himself, though. "It didn't surprise me a bit," Shaw said. "They made plays at the end to win, we didn't. I want to congratulate him. I wanted to do it face-to-face but I'll send him a note . . . They're good, they have an outstanding player in No. 90 (George Uko), and No. 94 (Leonard Williams) is outstanding . . . Dion Bailey, Devon Kennard . . . That's the shame of their season, their injuries, it happens all over the country . . . we went through it a couple of weeks ago . . . but they had a chance to come back healthy."

And they played like it.

"This is something we wanted for the past Trojans and coaches that fought hard," Vainuku said, "this is for the Trojan family."

28

A Rose Bowl for the ages as Sam steps up

The problem with USC's record-shattering come-from-behind 52–49 Rose Bowl win in 2017 over Penn State was the fact that you literally did not know where to turn when Matt Boermeester's 46-yard game-winning field goal split the uprights as time ran out.

Which way to go? Whom to hug first? USC all-time Hall of Famers Marcus Allen and Ronnie Lott and President Max Nikias, as well as senior tackle Zach Banner, were all trying to figure it out, as well. No one had a clue which way to turn. But they all knew how to shout and smile and find someone to congratulate after a win that was more than surreal. It was simply overwhelming.

Did that really happen? Did a Trojans team that trailed, 49–35, against the Big Ten champs with less than 9:00 left as day turned into night in Pasadena really just pull that off, really just score the last 17 points? And did a Nittany Lions team that scored touchdowns on 4 straight offensive plays in the second and third quarters and on 7 straight possessions actually lose this game? Is that possible? Can a defense that almost leaves the stadium for half the game possibly find a way to win?

USC did. And it did so in a way that assistant coach John Baxter, back after a year at Michigan, says makes USC so special. What he had missed most, Baxter said, was "the best motto in all of sports—'Fight On'. . . . You can't say that or do the sign when you're not at USC."

But USC did more than sing it or signal it. They made it come alive. They lived it. They played through it. They showed the crowd of 95,128 exactly what it means. "It's the will to win that Sam Darnold has," Marcus Allen said with a shake of his head at the redshirt freshman whose record 5 touchdown passes on 453 passing yards [473 overall]

Sam Darnold escaing a Penn State defender in his record-breaking game, leading the Trojans to a 52–49 comeback in the 2017 Rose Bowl against the Nittany Lions.

put his name at the top of the Rose Bowl record book. The best part of those 473 yards of total offense is how they erased the previous Rose Bowl record of 467 by Texas's Vince Young in a 2006 matchup USC fans would rather not remember.

But it wasn't all offense as much as the scoreboard might indicate. No one had a bigger smile that day than senior safety Leon McQuay III, who went out of Troy as the big winner. Sure, he dropped a possible game-winning interception. But he then followed it up with another on the next play that set up the win. At that point, he was ready for it. When Boermeester kicked the game-tying extra point with just 1:20 left, all he could think was *Get back out there and stop them.*

The USC defense did even better than that—it got the ball back for Darnold & Co. As unprepared as the USC defense appeared for so much of the second and third quarters, it was ready at the end. "You shake it off," Leon said of his first missed interception. "And then he gave me another chance . . . he tried to look me off but I didn't go for it," Leon said. He went for the ball instead. And the rest, as they say, is history—and hugs.

"Who's got the hats?" was all Leon could say immediately after the game. He wanted one of those "Rose Bowl Champs" hats. Asked for his explanation of what just happened, all he could say was: "I keep saying it. It's our motto: 'Fight On'. Some day—in a couple of years," Leon said, "I'll look back on this and say, 'Dang, that was big.'"

Another senior, linebacker Michael Hutchings, explained how a USC defense that gave up 49 points in the first 3 quarters managed to shut Penn State out in the fourth quarter. "The guys were playing for pride at that point . . . we knew we still had a chance. . . . Coach

Helton kept saying give me one more chance [for the offense] . . . all we tried to do was give them a chance."

For drama, come-from-behind excitement, and a finish fans will never forget, this is the game that's right up there with the "Bush push" win at Notre Dame in 2005. So much emotion. So many tears of joy. Such unabashed thrill of victory after coming so close to the agony of defeat. One reason this was so special was that the team that lost, Big Ten champion Penn State, was so well prepared and unwilling to give in itself. Saquon Barkley (194 yards, 2 touchdowns), Trace McSorley (18 for 29 passing for 254 yards and 4 TDs), and Chris Godwin (9 catches, 187 yards, 2 TDs) performed even better than their reputations. But as many answers as Penn State Coach James Franklin & Co. seemed to have, they didn't have enough.

Not for this USC squad on this day in this stadium where so many special things have happened for a USC football team winning its record twenty-fifth Rose Bowl. "It says we're back," Banner said simply, one of the few USC survivors from an ugly postgame fight in the 2012 losing Sun Bowl locker room after a game as far from this as it's possible to play. "That wasn't USC football," Banner said of the game five years prior. This was, for a USC team that after starting 1–3 would finish up with nine straight wins and ranked as the nation's No. 3 team in the final AP Poll. "We earned it," he said. "We earned the win in this game—and all the other stuff."

Director of Athletics Lynn Swann sounded a note of caution amid all the celebration. "We're not there yet, it's a building process." But USC's 52 points eclipsed all its previous 33 Rose Bowl games. "That's a great football team," Penn State's Franklin said.

Darnold was named the game's Outstanding Offensive Player after his 10-for-10 passing in the final quarter. Then when USC most needed it, the Trojans got a game-high 8 tackles from the game's Outstanding Defensive Player, Stevie Tu'ikolovatu, a first-year grad student transfer from Utah who went through a full season's tough times this past September. He also "Fought On."

Adoree' Jackson finished his last USC game on the bench with a high ankle sprain, but the All-American defensive back had the right question afterward. "Can we talk about Deontay Burnett?" Adoree' asked of his fellow Serra High alum. All the slim sophomore did was pull in career-highs for catches (13)—a Rose Bowl record—as well as yards (164) and, most important, touchdowns (3), including the game-tying 27-yarder with 1:20 left concluding a 5-play, 80-yard, game-tying drive in :39 that was Sam's "coolest" moment of a day filled with them, according to ABC's Kirk Herbstreit. And yes, he did hear the ear-piercing cheer that came with it. "I did," Deontay said. "I ran right up to our fans and found my family and signaled them."

The signal? "Fight On," of course, as he flashed that two-fingered "V" for victory. It was the universal theme. If the USC fans had known that the route he ran wasn't the route he was supposed to run and the ball was supposed to go to someone more shallow, they'd have cheered louder. "That's Deontay," Darnold said. "That's just the player he is. He made a play and I saw him."

And then on came Boermeester. "I knew I was going to kick it as soon as Leon intercepted it. He ran right by me." And so on the field where his father, Peter, was a star, but for UCLA and not in the Rose Bowl, he got the ultimate kick. "You want to be the guy who gets to kick it," Matt said of his Rose Bowl record-tying third field goal. And so he was.

Special teams coach Baxter had told him to stay with his routine. And so he did. He didn't even know how far it was. "It doesn't matter," he said. "You kick them the same way." But it mattered to his dad, waiting right outside the locker room. The elder Boermeester, who "teed it up for me my first kick down in La Jolla," Matt said, "was still in a state of shock. I could tell he'd been crying."

He wasn't alone. "That game doesn't really define us," Penn State's Franklin said. "I wouldn't be any more proud tonight sitting here with a win . . . after what might have been the most exciting Rose Bowl game ever."

Said USC Coach Clay Helton: "It was just two really good football teams playing at the highest level and competing until the absolute, very end," Helton said. "The greatest players shined brightest on the biggest stage. It's what fairy tales are made of."

It was more than that, Helton felt. "These kids are the definition of 'Fight On,' whether it was the season or the game."

In the 2017 Rose Bowl, it was both.

29

Jake Olson, miracle Trojan

It was the perfect moment and a miracle all in one for a USC football program that had seen its share of both of those. But none like this.

It took just seconds in real time, so quick that many in the sweltering Coliseum crowd of 61,125 that September 2, 2017, day had no idea it was happening. They were just trying to get through the 98-degree heat in a 49–31 season-opening USC win over Western Michigan.

And then it was over. USC had the final points in a surprising struggle of a game. The Trojans had even called a timeout to kick that last extra point to get it to 49 and an 18-point win. But then why all the celebrating on the sidelines—and from the student sections right behind the bench and those folks in the end zone? What was the source of the sheer joy of all those USC football players? Where was that coming from?

Some people knew. Some others had to know. Western Michigan Coach Tim Lester knew. He'd gone along with a deal USC Coach Clay Helton had offered him a couple of days earlier. USC wouldn't rush the Broncos' first extra point attempt that day if the Broncos would return the favor later—if USC needed one.

And as it turned out, after a late-breaking Marvell Tell interception for a touchdown, USC would need the favor, leading 48–31. "I didn't think it was a hard decision at all," Lester told *USA TODAY*. "It was bigger than the game. I was happy to be a part of it."

He wasn't the only one. But at the time, Jake Olson's parents weren't sure how to feel. They knew it was a possibility that their son, blind after a second surgery to remove his right eye when he was twelve for retinoblastoma and after losing his left eye first to the rare cancer at the age of ten months, might play. And yet, sightless for the last eight years, Jake might actually take his place on the turf of the historic Coliseum for the No. 4 Trojans, his all-time favorite team. It was a possibility. It was something he'd been working for since entering USC in 2015, something he'd been thinking about since that day when visiting former USC Coach Pete Carroll invited him to Seattle for a Seahawks practice after the surgery that took his sight.

That's when Seahawks snapper Clint Gresham had asked Jake, then fourteen, if he had any interest in doing what Gresham did. "He showed me how to grip the ball and gave me the sense of how to release the ball," Jake told John Feinstein of the *Washington Post*. "It was amazing. I realized this was a way for me to keep playing football."

And here he was, about to play football for real. But his parents weren't sure until fans sitting in the stands pointed it out to them that indeed, it was for real. In fact, Jake had thought it would happen in the first half that day, if it was to happen at all. But Western Michigan would have none of it, challenging the No. 4 Trojans on every play. So Jake thought his time had passed on this day when he heard the crowd and the score for Martell's TD with 3:13 left in the game and USC ahead, 48–31, at the time. Then Jake heard his holder, Wyatt Schmidt, telling him it was go time. Jake wasn't as loose as he'd have liked. But he was off, hand on Wyatt's shoulder pads.

"There's Jake," the person sitting next to Cindy Olson, Jake's mom, and his dad, Brian, shouted. Indeed, it was. By now, the TV announcers were trying to figure out why the timeout for USC. Then they realized it was to allow time for Jake to trot out onto the field, to get set for this one small but more than special proof of the triumph of the human spirit.

And for Lester to tell his Western Michigan team what was going on. USC had backed off the first extra point, they would back off now. "It was cool to watch it happen," Lester told *USA TODAY*. "Just to see the reaction on their sideline, you could see how big it was for them."

But not just for the USC coaches and players, or the fans who figured it out, but for the whole country. Jake was the biggest story in all the national media out of college football's first weekend. Jake has been to New York for ESPN and ABC to tell his story, which he will tell you is part of the reason he does what he does. Although there's another part: he loves football, loves being part of a team, loves USC, and most of all, stubbornly he says, loves anything that challenges his resiliency.

"I'll never tell anyone that life is fair," Olson has said of the loss of his sight. "Everyone is dealt with an unfair set of cards in some way . . . but I do tell them that at the end of the day, it's your decision." It is a message he delivers in as many venues as he can as a motivational speaker and in the book he coauthored—*Open Your Eyes: Ten Uncommon Lessons to Discover a Happy Life.*

Joining his Trojans teammates, Jake Olson "Fights On" in a postgame salute in front of the
USC marching band.

"To sit there and feel sorry for myself and be angry . . . it would be pathetic," Jake says. "It would hold me back in life. I really wanted to make sure that blindness and going through cancer was not going to stop me . . . and so, being grateful is another thing that really just helped me move on to accept my reality of not being able to see."

Jake's book expresses his philosophy of life. And so here he was. This had been a long time coming. Since the day when Jake, a USC fan all his young life after bonding with those Pete Carroll teams that had invited him in when Pete learned of Jake, had chosen to spend his last sighted day at a USC practice in 2009. It was heartwarming, to see the love of USC football from Jake, and the love from USC football players and coaches for Jake.

It was also incomprehensibly sad for all those there that day who had been accustomed to seeing the gangly blond preteen from Huntington Beach with those big glasses at USC practices. And knowing that this practice was the last one Jake would ever see. It kind of took your breath away, the immensity of it.

Little did anyone know the half of what would follow that moment. Maybe Jake would not see another practice, but people would see Jake—first as a much-more-grown-up young man at Orange Lutheran High School, one of Southern California's top prep football programs, where he won a spot as a long-snapper after thousands of hours of dedicated hard work and an athletic body cooperating to let him play the one position Jake knew he didn't have to be sighted in order to play.

He just had to be determined and disciplined—and then he had to be able to do it. But doing it at the high school level for two years is one thing. Doing it at USC, for one of the nation's historic programs in a season when the Trojans were shooting for a spot in the College Football Playoffs, was another.

That would take some doing. First it would take one of USC's "Swim with Mike" scholarships for handicapped athletes. Then it would take an NCAA waiver allowing Jake to accept that scholarship and still play football and not count against the 85 scholarships permitted by NCAA rules. The NCAA gave Jake its blessing and the waiver.

With that accomplished, it would take unwavering determination by Jake, who can be seen on a daily basis making his way to the John McKay Center, home of USC football, with his guide dog, Quebec, to get ready for practice. It is there that Trojans players and staff members take turns getting Jake through his practice paces.

Though it's not often the word one uses in a football setting, there was something "lovely" going on. The love, the teamwork, the pride—Jake was inspiring it. He was also inspiring his coach, Clay Helton, in his second year of bringing the message of "Faith, Family, and Football" to the Trojans program, to say they were going to make it happen, just as Jake was making it happen—with the help of his teammates. It was the ultimate team-building exercise, and it was being driven by a young man, all grown up now at 6-foot-4 and 235 pounds, who last saw a USC practice when he was twelve.

But even if he can't see them, Jake never misses a practice—not for the last two years. Like with his long snaps. They have to be perfect. In 1.2 seconds, the ball has to be back to the holder and placed perfectly for the kicker, in this case another Orange County guy, Chase McGrath, to knock it through the uprights. Which is exactly what happened that day, September 2, 2017.

Although if fans were looking for a special moment, what was so special here is how it wasn't so special. Just another perfect extra point. Just what they practiced. Just the way the kicker does it. Just the way Jake wanted it. And yet . . .

And yet, imagine the pressure for Jake. This was the result of eight years of dreaming and planning and practicing and hoping. An accomplished public speaker as a national advocate for people that they can achieve their dreams, not to mention a published author with two books to his name and an accomplished golfer who can shoot in the seventies when he has the time for it, had put it all on the line. How important was that snap? It was everything Jake had ever worked for and dreamed about and now there were all those teammates a part of the Olson family.

But not once did any of that show on his face. This was business as usual. This was practice as usual. This was just the way the kicker does it.

"What a pressure player," Helton said after the game. "Is that not a perfect snap at that moment? It's beyond words."

And then the world realized what had just happened. One after another, both LA and national sports and news media—print, TV, radio, and social media—jumped on Jake's train. ESPN's Shelley Smith got there first even though her network wasn't televising the game. But she'd built up a connection with Jake from stories she'd done with him eight years ago. And from her own connection with twelve-year-old Jake inspiring her after her own bout with breast cancer.

Jake explained it all a few days later in a letter to ESPN. Did he ever think this was possible? "The short answer to that question: No."

And yet here he was doing just that. "How in the world could I have expected this?" Jake wrote. "When I was twelve and about to lose my eyesight," how he would brush his teeth, do his homework, and be independent were the things Jake said he was thinking about. "Playing football became my last priority."

Talking of his "inherent stubbornness," Jake said that learning about resilience has been one of the most important lessons for him. And for those skeptical of "a blind kid playing football," Jake said he couldn't blame them. When he first started snapping, "I sucked."

But that's where the Jake story, instead of stopping, just got started. His high school coach, Dean Vieselmeyer, stayed with him. Then USC came through with the scholarship, and USC Director of Athletics Pat Haden and Associate AD J.K. McKay encouraged Jake to come out for football. "The day I was accepted to USC was one of the happiest days of my life," Jake said. "It was my dream school."

And now at a linebacker-sized 235 pounds on his no-longer-skinny 6-foot-4 frame, with two years of work behind him at USC, Jake knew he was getting close. But when Helton and special teams coach John Baxter talked to him about it, "I told them bluntly I wanted them to put me in only if I had earned the opportunity." That's when Helton told him he had, Jake said, causing him two sleepless nights after hearing those words the Thursday before the opener. And then it looked like it was a no-go. The game was too close. Until that pick six.

"I didn't feel as prepared as I would have liked," Jake said of the sudden sideline reversal. "But I knew I was ready."

From there, things materialized the way they practice it every day. Ball goes down. Kick goes up in 1.2 seconds. Perfect. That's why you practice. And that was it, right? Not exactly. "What came next was something I could never have contemplated," Jake said. "The insane outpouring of love and support—from my teammates, my family and friends, USC fans, and really everyone in general—was something I will treasure for a lifetime. It means the world to me that I have inspired others to pursue their dreams."

But there are other goals, Jake says. He'd like to snap against a live rush and play on the PGA Tour, if he can. And mainly just keep on inspiring others.

30

At long last, Troy takes home a Pac-12 title

By profession, USC President Max Nikias is an engineer, an academician, a researcher, and a teacher—not a sportswriter. But he got the lede exactly right after the Trojans won their first Pac-12 football championship December 1, 2017, ending a tough seven NCAA-sanctions-limited seasons.

"That was every game we played all year," Max said after USC's way-closer-than-it-should-have-been 31–28 win over recent nemesis Stanford, the second time the Trojans had handled the Cardinal in 2017. "And we won," Max said.

Indeed, as it has been for these Trojans, improving to 11–2 and hoping to make a run at the College Football Playoffs, they made their fans—including their president—hold their breath all the way to the finish line. "I need a big hug," Max said with a grin as expansive as all of Santa Clara's Levi's Stadium, where the full-blown celebration was just getting started.

The Trojans had taken a step past where they'd gone a year ago. Sure, that USC team made it to the Rose Bowl, where it beat Penn State, 52–49, in one of the great Rose Bowls of all time. But it stumbled when it came to the conference championship. So maybe it was one small step forward, taking home a Pac-12 title, but it was going in the right direction.

But there was a second, maybe larger step, as well for USC in beating Stanford twice in a season after having lost seven of the previous nine games to the Cardinal coming into this season, including USC's only other trip to the title game in 2015 when the Trojans got smoked, 41–22.

Not this time. But not to get carried away here. If there were some sort of Silicon Valley digital gizmo that could condense a team's twelve regular-season games into a single

Clay Helton and his Trojans enjoyed USC's first-ever Pac-12 football championship trophy in 2017 after beating Stanford.

sixty minutes, this was it. It included all the peaks and valleys, the joys and frustrations, the answered questions and the unanswered, the head-slappers and the back-slappers, the great plays—and those others.

The miracle here is that USC once again, as it did against Texas and Utah, Cal and Colorado, even UCLA and Western Michigan, found a way—or several of them—that let it walk away a winner when it mattered most at the very end. Only once—at Washington State with five starters out on the short end of back-to-back-week road trip on a Friday— did they falter in a game where they had a chance at the end.

No faltering this time. Some semifaltering, maybe. That was the 2017 Trojans' way. But there was no complete stumble. And for a night, it didn't matter, which explains why there was a kind of joy no one had seen around a USC football team—well, since last New Year's Day. And yet this was unlike anything we've seen this season—or last. Because the trophy gave it permanence.

"This is the game I'll remember," quarterback Sam Darnold said when asked to compare it to the Rose Bowl after completing 17 of 24 passes for 325 yards and 2 touchdowns while leading USC to the game-winning 99-yard touchdown drive in just 3:28 with under

4 minutes left. That's what it took for a three-point victory over a tough-minded, physical Stanford team that, under David Shaw, had defeated the last two Top Ten teams it had played the previous three weeks—Washington and Notre Dame.

"We're champions," Sam said simply. They were, indeed. Though arguably USC should not have put itself into a position to have to defend a dozen Stanford plays from the 33-yard line after a 30-yard punt from out of the end zone in the fourth quarter, and then even more perilously, 7 Stanford plays from a first and goal at the 3, it made the play—or plays—it had to make.

As USC discovered, one cannot stop Stanford's power-running ground game seven times on two possessions starting at the three-yard line. No one does, especially with the lead and the Pac-12 title on the line. And then it happened. After losses, penalties, stops, and yards given up grudgingly, Stanford was at the USC two with two plays left. Yet twice inside the one-yard line, USC stood strong.

"I got the first one," senior defensive tackle Josh Fatu said. "And Uchenna [Nwosu] got the second," he said of the second senior to stand strong at the goal line in the last regular season game either would play for the Trojans.

But nothing would top Nwosu's play, capping both a sensational final season and a USC career. The 6-foot-3, 245-pound edge defender was lined up outside the Stanford tight end on the right side. "But I'd seen that formation on film," he said. They were going the other way. Straight power outside the opposite tackle, he recognized. Uchenna would have to get there somehow. And as so often with the nation's quickest defender off his feet defending passes at the line of scrimmage, Nwosu got into his sprinter's stance—and somehow got there, crossing behind six Stanford O-linemen and a fullback at the snap. And before Cameron Scarlett reached the line of scrimmage, a diving Nwosu had him by the ankle. In the backfield. Not only did Scarlett come up short of the goal line, he would not quite reach the line of scrimmage.

"That was huge," USC linebacker Cameron Smith said of the defensive stop. "It feels so good, especially against Stanford, who thrives on that stuff. We made a play when the team needed it." No touchdown. USC ball. Still a USC lead with 8:00 left. Which became more important after Darnold and Jones would combine to lead USC on that length-of-the-field scoring drive, using up four minutes for a 31–21 lead that would stand up against a desperation final Stanford aerial charge.

"Do you know where I could get one of those caps?" Fatu asked of the championship gear USC was already passing out. This one clearly meant a lot to these guys. As it should have. But like almost always, they didn't make it easy on themselves.

Nor did Stanford. Thirty times USC's Ronald Jones had to carry the ball for his 140 yards (a 4.7 average) in order to outdo Heisman candidate Bryce Love's 125 on 22—although the Stanford All-American was doing it on a bad ankle. "That was hard," RoJo said of the numbers that moved him past O.J. Simpson into the No. 5 spot on USC's all-time career rushing list with 3,555 yards to O.J.'s 3,423. Although on the game's decisive score, RoJo would glide effortlessly into the end zone on an 8-yard sweep right past Stanford defenders with no chance to stay with him. "You liked that one?" he asked media quizzing him about it. All of Trojan Nation liked it.

"Lordy, God and a great bunch of kids," were USC Coach Clay Helton's first post-game words. "I couldn't be more proud of them. . . . We said failure was not an option." Although there were times it seemed like it might be as Stanford, despite the lopsided stat sheet in favor of USC, edged closer and closer thanks to USC's ill-timed penalties and poorly played deep coverage situations on jump balls where the Trojans had people in place to make plays.

"And we just didn't [fail]," Clay said. No, they didn't. And for a second time in the 2017 season, not only did they beat Stanford, they drubbed them with more than 500 yards of offense (501 to be exact after a record 623 against the Cardinal in Week Two) to Stanford's 343. So maybe it shouldn't have been all that close in a story USC fans had seen play out for much of 2017.

One reason for that was USC sophomore wide receiver Michael Pittman, finally all the way back from a high ankle sprain that cost him half of the season and then some. Finally, the 6-foot-4, 215-pounder would show what he could do. And show he did. His 146 receiving yards set a Pac-12 championship game record as he recorded career highs in yards and with his 7 catches. The most noteworthy catch was a game-changing 54-yarder as Sam spotted him from the USC goal line on that final drive to flip the field in a way only a play like that could have done.

That play was offensive coordinator Tee Martin's favorite play call. "I almost talked myself out of that one . . . but I didn't," Tee said of the bomb from the end zone that took some guts to go with—and maybe even more guts to throw.

Which was why Darnold, the game's MVP, was sought out afterward by Gen. David Petraeus, a USC Widney Professor, in his USC jacket as a guest of President Nikias. "He has ice water in his veins," Petraeus said of Darnold. "He just doesn't get nervous when those big plays come." No, he doesn't. But USC fans were plenty nervous, as they should have been, and as they had been much of the year. Once again, however, USC did not make them sad.

Nervous, yes. Sad, not so much. The Trojans were Pac-12 champions—at last. And feeling pretty good about it.

Epilogue

The anticipation continues to be high, and thus the challenges great, for USC football to keep producing teams that can compete for Pac-12 championships and Rose Bowl berths almost every year, with national championships coming along every so often. Those expectations will not change.

What will change, and already has, may be USC's ability to compete. The program has had the ability, as history makes clear, to compete with anyone—if it has a great coach. And it will do just that now and in the near future. Not that it will be as simple or straightforward, maybe, as it had been in the past.

The Pac-12 Conference has been falling behind—and to a certain extent, USC has been falling with it. Conferences matter more than ever now. When the Big Ten and the Southeastern Conference, even the Big 12, are pulling away from the Pac-12 in terms of up to $20 million per team per season in TV money, this is becoming more of a challenge even for a USC program with a number of the highest-rated TV games in college football history on its résumé.

Given the impact of big money on college football, there are more contenders than ever for the top rung, the place that USC has reached 11 times in its history. Alabama, Ohio State, Georgia, Clemson, and Oklahoma all seem committed, with the resources and coaching, to be in the mix almost every year. Texas, Notre Dame, Washington, Penn State, Stanford, Florida State, LSU, and Michigan appear to be waiting in the trenches.

The number of teams that USC must compete with to reestablish itself on the top rung of college football has expanded from the days of John McKay and even Pete Carroll.

The amount of resources being marshalled to get there is also increasing. USC's ability to keep up will be challenged like never before.

And yet, USC is in a position—in Los Angeles and on the West Coast—to be that dominant outsider it has always been since the mid-1920s when Hall of Famer Howard Jones headed West. As a top-25 academic institution with a campus packed with gleaming new buildings, all it needs is a program-defining coach.

Clay Helton's 21 wins in 2016 and 2017 are the most of any USC coach his first two seasons at Troy, although teams can play 14 games now instead of the 10 or 11 in earlier seasons. But add to that a Rose Bowl championship after the 2016 season and a Pac-12 title in 2017, along with recruiting classes that have kept USC in the top three in the nation with Alabama and Ohio State, and this should be a time of optimism for the Trojan nation.

But it's not—at least not exactly. One-sided losses to Notre Dame in South Bend and to Ohio State in the 2017 Cotton Bowl, plus a Friday night road loss at Washington State that eliminated, for all practical purposes, USC from the College Football Playoffs chase in September after opening the season as a favorite to get there, have the Trojans fan base a bit uneasy.

Is Clay Helton the right man for the job? Sure, he can recruit 'em, but can he coach 'em up? Can he be the visionary program-builder Jones was? The tough-minded battler McKay was? Or the inspirational competitor that Carroll was?

Those aren't the only questions facing this Trojans program. Does USC remain in a 12-team conference that seems to only be doing worse in the race for the TV dollars and football relevance at the bottom end? Or does it look elsewhere?

Then there's the famed Los Angeles Memorial Coliseum, USC's home since 1925. Now the United Airlines Memorial Coliseum, it's begun a controversial two-year renovation that will greatly expand the luxury suites and private boxes in a tower structure on the old press box side while removing 10,300 seats there for the 2019 season. That the new downsized Coliseum, with its wider aisles and deeper seating rows when completed, will drop to a capacity of 77,500 from 93,607 is the cause of some consternation among long-time USC ticket holders displaced from their prime seating.

There is another issue. The NFL is back in LA, with two teams, even, with the return of the Rams in 2016 and the relocation of the Chargers in 2017. And both return to a brand-new $5 billion stadium complex in Inglewood in 2020. That's some serious competition USC has not had to face for fans and media attention since the Rams left for St. Louis in 1994.

For many years, Los Angeles had been a USC town. It still could be. LA loves a winner, as USC has shown whenever it has won and won big. But that's the key.

All USC has to do is win—and win big.

Just like always.

After all, with so much that's changed, nothing really has.